LORD HOWE ISLAND
RISING

Daphne Nichols

Front Cover: Neds Beach

Back Cover: Blinky Beach

Both photographed by Richard Morris,
courtesy of LHI Historical Society

Copyright © Daphne Nichols
Lord Howe Island Rising
ISBN: 0 - 646 - 45419 - 6

Distributed by Tower Books
Unit 2/17 Rodborough Road
Frenchs Forest NSW 2086

4-8 Gwynne Street
Richmond Victoria 3121
t +61 3 9429 1299
www.bondimaging.com

Printed and Published in Australia 2006
BA Printing & Publishing Services
1 Ethel Avenue Brookvale NSW 2100
Ph: (02) 9905 6144
sales@baprinting.com.au

INDEX

FOREWORD

When Daphne told me of her plans for this book I marvelled at her courage.

Researching and writing one's own family history is challenging enough but extending that to everyone's family is something else! It is a brave soul indeed who endeavours to capture the essence of *any* small community – let alone Lord Howe Island.

As a fellow native of Lord Howe, and understanding the fierce pride of Island families regarding their individual heritage, I appreciate the enormity of the task. Such a social history of the Island has never been written before.

There is something about being a Lord Howe Islander that engenders an emotional attachment, a sense of ownership and belonging that defies explanation. For me the Island is not only the most beautiful place in the world but is essentially my 'sacred place'. Home is not just the lovely old timber house with all its memories that my grandparents built – 'home' is Lord Howe Island itself.

The author, whose family boasts a longer residence than mine, has encapsulated the key contributing factors in each family's history. But more than that it is a remarkable story of a small island and its people, and how they found their place in the world. 'Lord Howe Island Rising' is a valuable record for Islanders, their extended families and the many visitors who return to the Island annually.

Importantly, the book also notes the success of our forebears in preserving the Island's unique flora, fauna and marine life. I can only hope that today's intensive management, much of it from afar, is not detrimental and that future generations can enjoy Lord Howe Island as we have.

Beyond all this, Daphne has provided us with a damned good read!

Rosemary Sinclair AO

The Beginning

An undersea plateau extends approximately 1600 km north-west from the centre of the South Island of New Zealand. At that point it heads north another 1400 km to the Chesterfield Reefs midway between New Caledonia and the Queensland coast.

About 80 million years ago this 300 km wide plateau, known as the Lord Howe Rise, formed part of the Australian mainland until movement of the Earth's crust caused its separation.

The western edge of the Rise is bounded by a chain of flat-topped undersea volcanic mountains called guyots. Over 6 million years ago one erupted and, from a fiery lava lake, an island paradise was born.

For millennia this tiny slice of creation played host to an exotic array of marine, animal, plant and bird life from a forgotten time – two majestic mountains watching over them like silent sentinels.

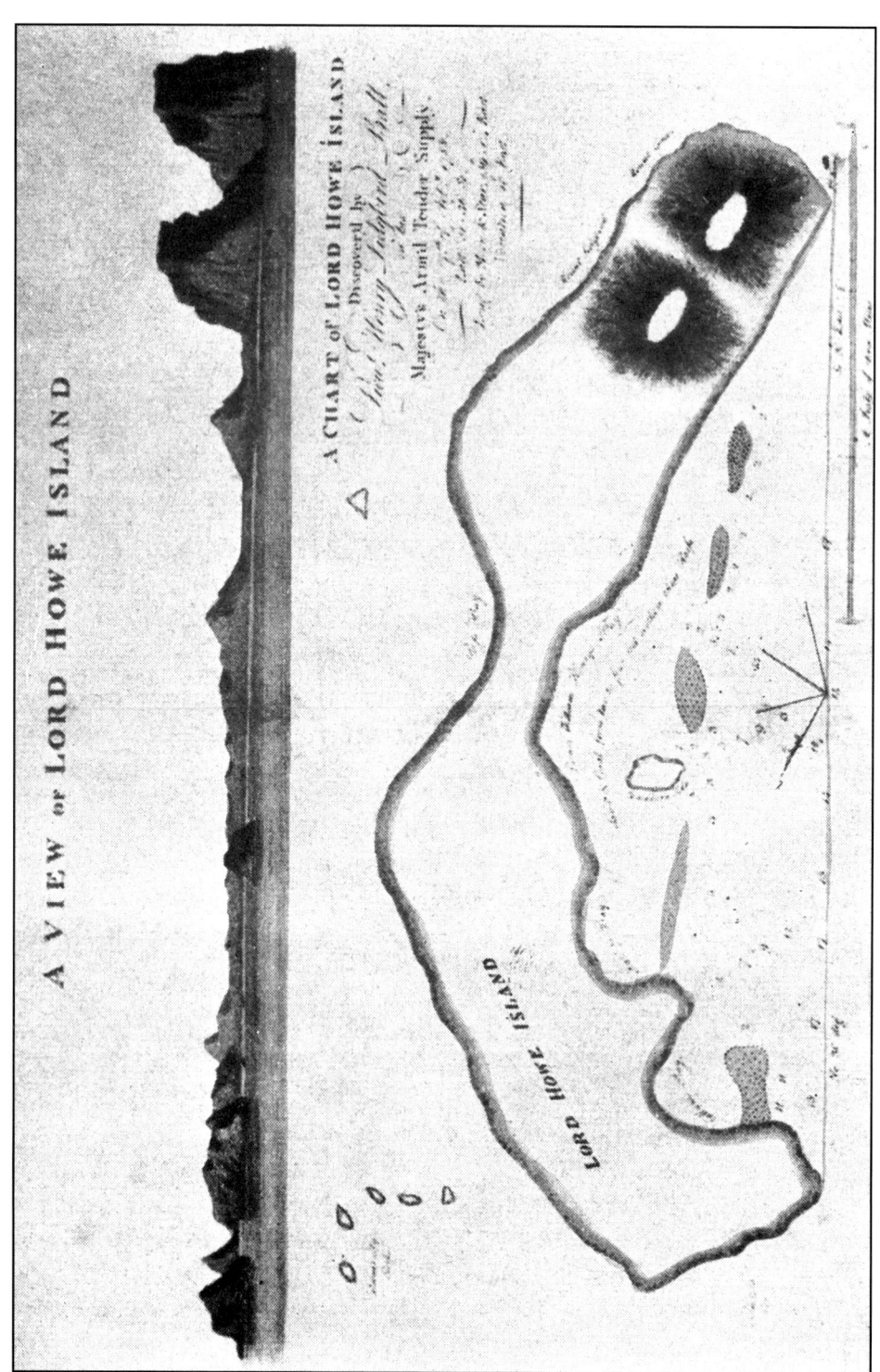

DISCOVERY

HMS Supply (sketch by Larry Wilson)

Lord Howe Island, a jewel on the World Heritage list, is the crescent-shaped volcanic remnant of a distant past. Just 11 km long and 2.8 km at the widest point, it lies in a southern arm of the Pacific Ocean – the Tasman Sea. The Island, surrounded by twenty-seven offshore islets and rocks including the spectacular pinnacle known as Balls Pyramid, is a dependency of New South Wales. This remote island group is 570 km from its nearest neighbour, mainland Australia.

THE FIRST FOUR YEARS – 1788-1792:

The British accidentally discovered Lord Howe Island in February 1788; just three weeks after the Crown colony of New South Wales was established, ten years before the discovery of Bass Strait, and thirty-seven years before the colony began separating into the states that make up Australia today. However, the Island's existence was suspected a month earlier. Navigator Jean Francois de Galaup La Perouse, as he was sailing to Botany Bay at the end of a three year expedition, wrote in his log: -

Le l7, par 3ld 28' de latitude Sud, et l59d l5' de longitude orientale, nous fumes environnes d'une innombrable quantite de goelettes, qui nous faisaient soupconner que nous passions aupres dequelque ile ou rocher; et il y ent plusiers paris pour la decouverte d'une nouvelle terre avant notre arrivee a Botany Bay….

The English translation is: -

On the seventeenth, situated at latitude 31°28 south and longitude 159°15 east, we were surrounded by an innumerable quantity of seagulls, leading us to believe that we were sailing near to some kind of island or rock; many of the crew members were speculating upon the discovery of New Land before our arrival at Botany Bay…

Had La Perouse made this discovery, it may well have been his last. Upon leaving Botany Bay on 12 March 1788 he and his men sailed into oblivion. Thirty-eight years later, wreckage of what was believed to be his two ships *La Boussole* and *L'Astrolabe* was discovered off an island in the New Hebrides. La Perouse and his men were immortalised in a 1959 book titled *The Vanishing Frenchman*.

Lieutenant Henry Lidgbird Ball, Commander of His Majesty's Armed Tender *Supply,* made the first sighting of the Island while en route to Norfolk Island from Port Jackson. He named it Lord Howes Island after Earl Richard Howe, a First Lord of the Admiralty from 1783 to 1788.

Richard Howe had a distinguished naval career beginning as Captain of a rated warship at the age of 20. He achieved early recognition for his defence of the English Channel in the Seven Years War; received a commendation for outmanoeuvring a superior combined Spanish and French fleet during the siege of Gibraltar; and was noted for his victory over the French in 1794 during the French Revolutionary Wars. Also known as Black Dick Howe he was created Earl and Baron Howe of Langar in 1788. He died in 1799 and was buried in the family vault at Langar, Nottinghamshire.

Henry Lidgbird Ball was born in England in 1757. He joined the Royal Navy at an early age and made the rank of Lieutenant in May 1779. Selected to join the First Fleet conveying convicts to New South Wales in 1787, he was given command of HMS *Supply.* After his return to England in 1792, Ball was promoted to Captain and served on various ships during the Napoleonic Wars. Wishing to return to New South Wales, he unsuccessfully applied for governorship of the Colony in 1808. Raised to the rank of Rear Admiral in 1814, Ball died in England on 23 October 1818.

Sailing with Lieutenant Ball on *Supply* were fifteen convicts (nine male and six female), and a detachment whose orders from Governor Arthur Phillip were to establish a penal colony at Norfolk Island. Philip Gidley King, 2nd Lieutenant on HMS *Sirius,* flagship of the First Fleet, was the leader of the expedition and the appointed Superintendent to the new colony.

The establishment of a penal colony lay in the desire of the British East-India Company (1600-1874) to exploit the tall Norfolk pine trees and the Island's flax. The company believed these commodities would diminish the great expense its Pacific cruising ships incurred in the supply of masts, spars, sail cloth, rope and cordage. Eventually, neither commodity was found to have the value the company envisaged; and upkeep of the remote island prison would become a strain on the resources of the settlement at Port Jackson.

On his return voyage from Norfolk, Lieutenant Ball landed a party on 13 March 1788 and took possession of Lord Howes Island in the name of his Britannic Majesty, King George III. At that time he named the following primary geographical features to reflect the newest of British territories in that age of discovery, or as some would call it today – invasion. The latter this history cannot equate to as there is no evidence of human habitation before 1788.

Prince William Henry Bay – William was the third son of King George III and reigned as King William IV from 1830 to 1837.

Blackburn Island – David Blackburn was Sailing Master of *Supply*.

Phillip Point, Phillip Bluff, Phillip Rock – Captain Arthur Phillip was appointed first Governor of the colony. In 1788 the territory of NSW extended from Cape York at the northernmost point of the continent, to the south cape of Van Diemens Land, inland for an indefinite distance; and included New Zealand.

Hunter Bay – Captain John Hunter was Commander of the flagship *Sirius*. He served as Governor of NSW from 1795 to 1800.

Callam Bay – James Callam was surgeon on *Supply*.

Collins Cove – Lieutenant-Colonel David Collins was Judge Advocate of NSW from 1788 to 1796. He founded the city of Hobart, Tasmania, in 1803.

Admiralty Islands – named after the British Admiralty.

Ross Bay – Major Ross was in charge of the military and convicts on *Supply*. He was later appointed Lieutenant Governor of Port Jackson.

Erskines Valley – Lord Thomas Erskine, a prominent defence lawyer who was appointed Lord Chancellor of England from 1806 to 1807.

King Point – Lieutenant Philip Gidley King was Superintendent of the Norfolk Island penal settlement from 1788 to 1800. He then served as Governor of NSW until 1806.

Mount Lidgbird and Balls Pyramid – named after Ball who described the latter as a 'pyramidical rock'.

Mount Gower – John Leveson Gower, First Marquess of Stafford. As a Lord of the Admiralty he served with Earl Howe during the siege of Gibraltar. He was raised to Rear Admiral in 1790.

Most of these landmarks are still identified by their original names. However, as settlement of the Island grew, some were changed to symbolise the Island's history since its discovery; while other features were named.

The Island was found to be abundant with birds, fish, turtles and coconuts but little other food sources, of which was written: -

> The principal vegetable produce of this island is the cabbage palm tree, bamboo, and mangrove with a curious specie of elder. In some places grows samphire, wild celery, cabbage, parsley, something like endive, and the grass is every where as sour as sorrel…

The cabbage palm is a name applied to several species whose young heads of tender leaves are cooked as vegetables. These include the palmetto, coconut and royal palm. Two varieties of palms abundant along the foreshore, and having never been seen before, were probably mistaken for cabbage palms; and the heads of the young ones referred to as cabbages. The wild celery and parsely are unknown today; and as the Island is situated too far south for coconut palms to grow more than a metre high (in which time the young tree can feed off the nut), the edible fruit of the pandanus tree may have been mistaken for a variety of coconut.

Lieutenant Ball did not consider the Island suitable as a subsidiary colony due to the difficulty in clearing the dense palm forests, the little value in its timber, the poor soil and the lack of anchorage for ships in Prince William Henry Bay. Instead, he felt its importance lay as a half-way provisioning stop between the infant settlements. Upon his return to Port Jackson with a quantity of live turtles weighing over 300lb (136kg) each, Ball conveyed to Governor Phillip: -

> The chief acquisition that we hope may accrue to our settlement from the falling in with

this island is the turtle, off which we hope to have many a feast

However, Lord Howe Island's use to the colony would be limited. Under orders issued by the Admiralty, prior to the First Fleet's departure from England, nine of the eleven ships set sail for various destinations leaving only *Sirius* and *Supply*. Also, the East-India Company's power and greed prohibited Governor Phillip from building any ships for the new colony. There was a risk, of course, that if a shipbuilding industry was established convicts might seize the vessels for escape. But foremost, the East-India Company feared a challenge to its monopoly. Thus the young colony, entirely dependent upon the sea for even the minimum necessities, and with 1500 km of ocean between its two settlements, was inhibited from developing its prime requirement – ocean transport.

On 17 May 1788 four transports lay at anchor off the south end of Lord Howe Island. Lieutenant Ball had been instructed by Governor Phillip to return on *Supply* to procure a further supply of turtles for the purpose of reducing scurvy, which was prevalent in the settlement at Port Jackson. The mission was unsuccessful as the turtle population had migrated to warmer waters for the winter months. The three other ships, *Lady Penrhyn, Scarborough* and *Charlotte* were en route to China under charter by the East-India Company to load tea for England. Journal entries made by officers on those vessels described in detail the myriad of beautiful birds and their habitat. Arthur Bowes, surgeon on the *Lady Penrhyn*, wrote: -

> When I was in the woods amongst the Birds I could not help picturing to myself the Golden Age as described by Ovid

It is interesting to note that in 1820 the Gilbert Islands (now part of the Republic of Kiribati) were named after Thomas Gilbert, Commander of *Charlotte*. Although partially discovered in 1606 by the Spanish, and in 1765 by British Vice Admiral and explorer, John Byron; it was on Captain Gilbert's voyage to China that he discovered seven more of the seventeen islands in the group, including Abemama. This island would later be the source of a family connection to Lord Howe Island spanning seven generations.

Just as Ovid's Golden Age of serenity, peace and eternal spring ended, so too would this idyllic paradise for a menagerie of bird life. For millennia they were free from predators, but with the arrival of man their lack of instinct for danger made them easy prey and a prized source of food. On 16 May 1788, Arthur Bowes wrote in his journal:-

> …the Ships Company came in the afternoon and stay'd on shore all night. The sport we had in knock'g down Birds, & ca. was great indeed tho' at the Expence of tearing most of the Cloathes of our backs. We made a fire under the trees and supp'd upon part of our game, broil'd wh. was very sweet and good, the Pidgeons were the largest I ever saw…

A great number of birds were slaughtered and the hunters were cruel in the pursuit of their prey, as suggested in the following journal entry by Captain Gilbert on the same date: -

> Great numbers of gannetts, very large and fat, were walking with less fear and concern than geese in a farmyard; and they were taken by hand, with much more ease. We found their nests in the long grass at the head of the beach, in each of which there were a great number of eggs, very large and well tasted when dressed. On entering the woods I was surprised to see large fat pigeons, of the same plumage and make as those in Europe, sitting on low bushes, and so insensible to fear, as to be knocked down with little trouble. Partridges likewise, in great plenty, ran along the ground, very fat, and exceedingly well tasted. Several of these I knocked down, and their legs being broken, I placed them near me as I sat under a tree. The pain they suffered caused them to make a doleful cry, which brought five or six dozens of the same kind of them, and by that means I was able to take nearly the whole of them. I might not otherwise have procured so many; for although they were by no means shy, yet they ran very fast when chased.

Over the next three years HMS *Supply* made further visits during the summer months in the search for turtles. After her return voyage to England in 1792, on which she carried a kangaroo as a gift for King George III, she was auctioned and renamed the *Thomas and Mary*. She was then used as a coal trader on the Thames until she went to the scrapyard in 1806.

Ships from the Second and Third Fleets to make landfall at Lord Howe included HMS *Gorgon, Mary and Anne, Salamander, Queen* and *Atlantic*. On voyages back to England via China for the lucrative tea trade, a tried and sure windship route took vessels northeast of Port Jackson to Lord Howe and Norfolk Island. From Norfolk they sailed north between New Caledonia and Fiji, crossing the equator at about longitude 173° E. Threading between the Marshall and Caroline Islands, the ships then turned west before the tradewinds to China and the Phillipines. When HMS *Gorgon* called at the Island on 26 December 1791 on her home voyage, James Scott, Sergeant of Marines, wrote in his journal: -

> Seen Houes Island. Got two boats out. Went on Shore, the officers Got Several Birds, I try'd every mains to procure a live Bird or two But could not obtain one. I offered one Guinea for a pair of live pidgons – the Boats Return'd Next day & we took our Departure

Government vessels continued to visit occasionally until 1814 when the penal colony at Norfolk was first disbanded. Lord Howe Island was still a long way off from settlement, but by then Australia's burgeoning fishing industry was bringing a new breed of mariner in search of its bounty. The whaling era had begun. One of the Colony's first whaleships to visit was the *Britannia*, which was believed lost on Middleton Reef in 1806.

However, from 1792 another 210 years would pass before the British navy again found Lord Howe Island – and again – quite by accident!

While 17 February is the accepted date of Lord Howe Island's discovery, conflicting times in journal entries made by Lieutenant Ball and Philip Gidley King give rise to speculation.

Lieutenant Ball's log entries stated: -

Feb. 17 Noon – Latitude 31° 36S – Longitude 159° 04E

Easterly. Moderate and cloudy. At a quarter past five p.m. saw two islands, bearing E.S.E. 18 or 19 miles distant. At noon the south end of the largest island bore S 68° E., the north end of the small one S 70° E., distant 15 miles. The largest was named Lord Howe's Island and the small one Lidgbird Island.

Feb. 18 Noon – Latitude 31° 40S – Longitude 159° 14E

Variable. Moderate and clear. At seven p.m. the body of Lord Howe's Island, E.S. 12 or 13 miles. Sounded no ground with 120 fathoms. Found the land seen on the 17th to be only one island. At noon it bore N.22 deg., four or five miles distant.

Philip Gidley King wrote: -

18th at Daylight Land was discovered bearing ESE & as we thought only 18 miles & took it for two small islands….at Noon had a very good Meridian Altitude which gave us 31°. 10'55"S°….at that time ye largest hill bore South 70°Et. On ye 19th at 4 in ye Morning having neared the Island considerably we sounded with 120 fathoms but no bottom. Found the two islands or hills that we had seen the day before, were two immense high rocky mountains, on ye South point of an Island. At Noon we had a very good Meridian Altitude by which our Latitude was 31°40'S° & ye Centre of the Island at that time bore from us N 30°Wt about 6 miles ….

The difference in dates can be partly explained in a reference from the *American Practical Navigator,* Bowditch, 1984: -

Nautical day defined…One complete revolution of the earth with respect to a celestial reference point is called a day. In modern usage every kind of solar time has its zero or starting point at midnight, when the celestial reference point is directly over the lower branch of the terrestrial reference meridian. This has not always been so. Until January 1, 1925 the astronomical day began at noon, 12 hours later than the start of the calendar day of the same date. The nautical day began at noon, 12 hours earlier than the calendar day, or 24 hours earlier than the astronomical day of the same date.

Although the British Navy adopted calendar time in 1805, during the Battle of Trafalgar, most official logbooks before 1 January 1925 were kept by nautical or 'ship time' with the day beginning at noon. The hours of pm preceded am and the latter was identical to the am of the calendar day or 'civil time'. Journals kept by supernumeraries on ships were written according to the calendar day. Also, until the end of the 19th century, there was no reference point from which voyagers took into reckoning a complete day change. This meant that as ships sailed west across the Pacific, all journal entries were one day less than modern dating.

As an example – the first sighting of Australia at Point Hicks, Victoria (now Cape Everard), by Captain James Cook is recognised today as 20 April 1770. Cook, using ship time, made the entry in his log at 6 am on 19 April, which was six hours before the end of the nautical day and six hours after the beginning of the calendar day of the same date. Joseph Banks, botanist on the HMS *Endeavour*, kept his journal by civil time, and his entry for the first sighting coincided with the date and time logged by Captain Cook. However, having sailed west across the Pacific and allowing for a day change, the sighting was on 20 April in modern dating.

A multiplicity of initial meridians were drawn on maps as early as the 17th century but it was not until the 1884 Washington Meridian Conference, represented by forty-one delegates from twenty-five countries, that a resolution selected the Greenwich meridian as zero or the common prime meridian for longitude. It was further resolved that from this meridian, longitude would be counted in two directions up to 180°; east longitude being plus and west longitude being minus. The exact course was never defined by any international treaty, law or agreement, but longitude 180° was designated as the International Dateline. Also, Resolution 6 of the Conference expressed the hope that, as soon as practicable, use of the nautical and astronomical days would cease.

Although the First Fleet sailed *east* across the Indian Ocean, an anomaly still exists with the discovery of Lord Howe Island. 5.15 pm in ship time on 17 February was also 5.15 pm in civil time on 16 February. The fact that King wrote *daylight on the 18th* suggests that Ball was using astronomical time with his day beginning at noon, twelve hours *after* the start of the calendar day. Curiously, his log entries for 17 and 18 February show only the hours of pm followed by noon. However, the distances he recorded from the Island match the daylight entries made by King on 18 and 19 February. This suggests Ball might have reversed the am and pm. Had he logged 5.15 am on 17 February, which in astronomical and calendar time was the morning of 18 February, both journals would have corresponded.

Balls Pyramid

11

2

SCURVY AND THE TURTLES

For the next 80 years the Island was an oceanic larder, a stop for scurvy ridden sailors heartily sick of British cooking (David Doubilet, National Geographic writer and underwater photographer)

Within three months of settlement the New South Wales colony was struggling to survive. Faced with famine and disease Governor Phillip was reluctant to divulge the exact location of Lord Howe Island to the departing nine vessels from the First Fleet; jealously guarding Lieutenant Ball's find as a provisioning port solely for Port Jackson. However, concerned with the rapid advance of scurvy among their men, the captains of the three ships heading to China were determined to find the Island to secure urgently needed supplies. Captain Gilbert of *Charlotte,* wrote: -

8th May 1788 – at 6.00am we weighed anchor and stood out of the harbour, breeze moderate westerly; at 7.30 with some difficulty we cleared the North and South Heads of Port Jackson and launched into the Pacific Ocean, where there were no charts to guide us, and dangers of which I was quite unaccustomed. Our ship was so small sized, and crew did not exceed thirty, several being boys. We stood to the N.E. in search of an island, which had been discovered by Lieutenant Ball on his passage to Norfolk Island. Having heard a very flattering account of this island and its produce,

White Swamp Hen (sketch by Surgeon Bowes)

I was determined to search strictly for it, although I had received only a hint as to its situation.

12th May 1788 – fearing from a conversation I had with Governor Phillip, when I took leave of him, that Captain Ball had directions to prevent my landing on this newly discovered island of promise, for that is the way Lord Howe Island was described at Port Jackson, as soon as it was dark I hauled to the north in order to avoid the 'Supply' and at the same time get into the latitude in which I supposed lay the island. The health of my ship's company rendered it necessary that I should, if possible procure a supply of fresh provisions and vegetables, especially as scurvy had begun to make rapid advance among them. I determined to surmount every difficulty and to land upon the island. At daybreak I was surprised to see the Brig close under my weather quarter. At 7am she stood E.N.E., and I concluded that Captain Ball did not choose to keep us company, lest it should be supposed that he conducted us to the island. So I kept my course without regarding him.

On 17 May 1788 *Charlotte, Lady Penhryn* and *Scarborough* found the *island of promise* and an abundance of fish and birds. However, they were disappointed that the fine green turtles they had heard so much about had migrated for the winter. Live turtles could be carried on board for extended periods thus providing fresh meat for part of their journey. It is not known how many men perished on those ships but when the *Friendship* and *Alexander* departed Port Jackson in July 1788, the deaths from scurvy eventually left the ships with insufficient men to crew them. With greater losses suffered on the *Friendship*, she was scuttled in the Straits of Macassar after her remaining crew transferred to the *Alexander*.

Scurvy had plagued man since the time of the Ancient World. The debilitating symptoms of this serious and too often fatal disease were described in Egyptian, Greek and Roman writings as early as 1500 BC. Predominantly a curse of mariners it reached epidemic proportions during the Age of Sail, an era beginning with European voyages of discovery in the late 15th century and ending with the development of steam power on ships in the mid 19th century. Long voyages in cramped quarters with poor sanitation and a diet of little else than salted meat, weevily biscuits and grog, saw an estimated two million sailors succumb in agony to this affliction.

Conquering the disease remained as elusive as its cause until 1747, when Scottish naval surgeon James Lind observed that something contained in citrus fruit counteracted the ravages of scurvy. Following a successful experiment in which he used oranges and lemons to treat patients on board HMS *Salisbury,* Lind began developing methods for the concentration and preservation of citrus juice at sea. Thus began trials of fruit, vegetables and other food sources that might contain the most effective antiscorbutic properties. Vitamin groups had yet to be identified, but scurvy became the first disease to be associated directly with a food deficiency.

When Captain James Cook commenced his decade long voyages in 1768, his concern for the health and welfare of his men prompted him to adopt the Admiralty's measures to prevent outbreaks of scurvy. He stocked his ships with a vast array of antiscorbutics, including concentrates of orange and lemon juice that were rationed daily to each man. He maintained a regimen of cleanliness, fresh air and a proper diet, which involved provisioning with fresh supplies whenever possible; and having the shipboard naturalists identify edible plants on foreign coasts.

In June 1770 HMS *Endeavour* was holed and trapped within the Great Barrier Reef. To save her Cook ordered nearly fifty tons of iron, stone ballast, six massive cannons and the spoiled provisions overboard, before guiding her into a sheltered estuary on the Endeavour River, known today as Cooktown. The crew remained there for seven weeks repairing the damaged hull. Fortunately, giant turtles swam in the lagoons, kangaroos dwelt in the scrub and antiscorbutic plants were abundant. Out of ninety-one souls, scurvy materialised in only one man and he soon recovered after living entirely on what he caught.

Ironically, on this three-year voyage from 1768 to 1771, Cook lost thirty-one men out of ninety-three but not one to scurvy – two were killed in New Zealand prior to the discovery of Australia, and twenty-nine succumbed to malaria and dysentery in Batavia on the journey home to England.

Scurvy was also a curse on land when there was a severe lack of fresh food and proper hygiene, as was the case with the new settlements at Port Jackson and Norfolk Island. For over two years the infant colonies would remain largely forgotten; and as famine threatened – diseases developed rapidly. When the promised supplies from England failed to arrive, Governor Phillip ordered Captain John Hunter to the Cape of Good Hope to seek provisions. Hunter departed on HMS *Sirius* in October 1788, sailing via Cape Horn, and returned in May 1789; a record circumnavigation for a relatively slow ship. However, the provisions he carried would offer only temporary relief.

Meanwhile, the Lord Howe Island turtles were deemed necessary in the colony's long fight for survival. Like the Galapagos tortoises providing sustenance for American and British whalers as they pushed into the Pacific towards the end of the 18th century, so too was the succulent meat of the herbivorous turtle considered high in nutritional value. Hunting parties were landed on the Island and generally remained two or three days; the longest recorded stay being fifteen days in January 1790. The quantity of turtles taken in a single expedition varied, and some did not survive the shipboard journey between Lord Howe, Norfolk and Port Jackson. The largest number captured was probably on Ball's return journey after the Island's discovery.

On 19 March 1788, James Scott wrote in his journal: -

> Between 20 & 30 turtel were procured which Capt. Ball supplied to the Officers
> Hospit'l

Procuring turtles was by no means an easy feat and depended on an element of
surprise. Awake, and in deep water, they were impossible to catch. Thus, the turtles
'turned' and rendered helpless were those sleeping on the surface of the sea close to
the beach. Harnesses were secured to the limbs of the larger ones to prevent them
from struggling against their captors as they were carried to the longboats.

The turtles captured during those summer months probably gave relief only to the
hierarchy, as suggested in Scott's journal on 19 March. The numbers were certainly
not enough to supplement the diet of the entire community. On 26 February 1790,
Governor Phillip ordered strict rationing to ease the ever-increasing burden. He also
ordered a division of the settlement by sending more marines and convicts to Norfolk
Island, under the command of Lieutenant Governor Major Ross.

On 6 March, Captain Hunter and Major Ross set sail on *Sirius* with a complement of
220 persons, including 186 convicts, and a proportion of Port Jackson's remaining
provisions. At the same time Lieutenant Ball embarked on *Supply* with a company of
marines and twenty convicts. Adding to the Governor's woes it was on this voyage
that *Sirius* was wrecked at Norfolk Island on 19 March. There was no loss of life but
the *Supply* was now the colony's only link to the outside world.

On 9 March, while en route to Norfolk on the fatal voyage of *Sirius,* Captain Hunter
made the following observation of Lord Howe Island: -

> We passed in the evening between the island and the pyramid, and had 26 fathoms
> within two miles of Mount Gower, over a rocky bottom. This island I judge to be
> about three miles and a half long, north-north-west and south-south-east; it is very
> narrow across. There is anchorage on both sides of it, but the bottom is foul. On the
> west side there is a bay, off which lies a reef parallel to the shore, with good swatches,
> or passages through for boats; this reef breaks off the sea from the shore, which is
> a fine sandy beach, so there is no difficulty in landing. I have observed before, that
> turtles are sometimes caught here, and that there are many birds upon the island.

An oasis lying between two struggling settlements! For better or worse, had more
ships been placed at the Government's disposal, Lord Howe Island may have played
a different role in the colony's establishment. But history dictated otherwise.

On 1 April 1790 the meagre rations of pork, rice and flour apportioned to each person at Port Jackson were reduced even further. These rations were all that remained of the First Fleet's stores on the voyage from England – the pork had been salted three or four years earlier; and the flour and rice were no more than moving bodies of weevils. Desperate wretches, grey with scurvy and wasted by starvation, struggled against the horrors of their situation. Death was everywhere. In desperation, Governor Phillip ordered Lieutenant Ball to Batavia on *Supply* in search of further provisions.

The first crops planted in 1788 had yielded little, deterring experimentation and further cultivation. Kangaroos, birds, snakes and lizards were added to the food chain whenever possible but esculent vegetables and wild fruits were almost non-existent. Supplies were exhausted, pilfering was rife, the Government had lost control and chaos reigned in the colony. As an officer observed in May 1790: -

> I am sorry to say this Government (if Government it can be called) is all anarchy and confusion – discontent and jealousy being evidently seen amongst the different heads of the settlement.
>
> Our soldiers have not a shoe and mount guard barefoot. Pride, pomp and circumstance of glorious war are at an end. So incessantly have we been employed that no military manoeuvre of the least consequence has been practised by us since our embarkment at Plymouth.
>
> An awful and terrible example of justice – six marines, the flower of our battalion – hanged by the public executioner for having at various times robbed the public stores.

The evening of 3 June 1790 brought a glimmer of hope when the first of six ships comprising the Second Fleet signalled her arrival. The elation within the colony was reflected by an officer of the day who saw fit to quote: -

> The first climax in our history has been passed

By the end of the month another four ships had laid anchor. However, the joy was short-lived as their arrival did little to relieve the human suffering. The fleet's ten-month voyage had been fraught with disaster. One of the victuallers, HMS *Guardian*, was forced to abandon the journey after she struck an iceberg in the North Atlantic losing most of her provisions. The first ship to arrive carried 222 women convicts, mostly aged or infirm and incapable of contributing to the colony's well-being. Of just over a thousand convicts on the four other ships, a quarter died on the voyage and half the remaining prisoners disembarked suffering from scurvy. The Reverend Richard Johnson remarked on the landing: -

> Great numbers were not able to walk, nor to move hand and foot; such were slung

over the shipside in the same manner as they would sling a cask …Some died upon deck and others in the boats before they reached shore …Some creeped upon their hands and knees and some were carried on the backs of others

In October 1790, *Supply* returned from Batavia *stocked with every necessary and conveniency* but, like the provisions carried on the Second Fleet, they offered only temporary relief. The ensuing summer brought hunting parties to Lord Howe Island, again in search of its turtles.

Conditions on the Third Fleet, which arrived between July and October 1791, were hardly better than those experienced in the Second Fleet. Subjected to meagre rations on ships that were stocked with ample provisions consigned for the colony, almost a third of the 1666 convicts were ill with scurvy on landing and a great number died. Nevertheless, the Third Fleet heralded a new beginning. By the end of 1791 a number of farmers had begun contributing to the colony. Although they had little more than a rudimentary knowledge of farming techniques, settlements at Rose Hill (now Parramatta) and the upper limits of Port Jackson were yielding better supplies of food, which in turn encouraged further cultivation, eventually bringing an end to famine and disease.

Crewmen on the Third Fleet also began the colony's first industry. On their voyage through Australian waters they had found an abundance of whales. Within days of unloading their human cargo the vessels' deckworks were rebuilt and whaling commenced along the coast. Pursuit of the whales brought new development and trade opportunities; and whale oil would become Australia's highest earning export commodity until the 1830s.

With the emergence of the whaling industry scurvy continued to curse mariners and Lord Howe Island would play a more important role as a provisioning port. In the early years, before fruit and other fresh produce were available on the Island, turtles were again prominent in supplementing the diets of men living on ships which, unlike the control measures eventually made mandatory on naval vessels, were inadequately stocked for long voyages. Scurvy sufferers were often put ashore and it seemed a common practice to initially cover themselves with warm sand, which supposedly offered temporary relief. Their survival then depended solely on what they caught and on any wild esculents they could find. However, for some who were hundreds or even thousands of miles from home, the Island or its surrounding waters became their eternal resting place.

Whether victims of scurvy or not, in 1915, evidence of what may have been several graves was found at the south end of the Island – unearthed by movement of sand and soil through the passage of time. Several artefacts including a ring, an octagonal earring and a small pipe with part of the stem broken off lay nearby. The bowl of the pipe was fashioned into a sailor's head complete with pointed beard and a peaked cap, which clearly bore the letters DEMOC SOC. Buttons believed to be from the uniform of a British soldier were also found at the entrance of a site known as Big Creek, now also called Soldiers Creek.

In the late 1970s a human skeleton was found at Old Settlement Creek at the northern end of the Island. It was stored, rather irreverently, in a cardboard box and for a decade lay in the Lord Howe Island Board's administrative offices before such action was considered inappropriate. The remains were finally sent to the Sydney Coroner's office. Old Settlement was also the burial site of Charles Brochar, cooper on the American barque *William Hamilton,* whose grave was marked by a piece of slate nailed to timber on 3 November 1840. Yet another life was claimed as late as 1873. Seventeen-year old Charles Chase, an American from the Nantucket whaling family of that name, died on 11 May that year. Possibly buried at sea, his death off Lord Howe Island is recorded in the Barney Genealogical Records of Nantucket.

After settlement commenced in the 1830s, shelter and a diet of fresh fruit and vegetables ensured the recovery of most scurvy sufferers, as was the case of the entire crew of the English brig *Genii* in 1840. From that time on some sailors, having recovered from the affliction, abandoned their life at sea choosing to make the Island their home. One was Ned Ambrim, an American, who remained on the Island for the rest of his life. He died on 6 June 1902, and his gravesite was one of the first recorded in the Island's public cemetery.

3

IN THE WAKE OF THE WHALES

The Whaler Aladdin after conversion to a gunpowder storeship, circa 1890

Five decades after its discovery, Australian, American, British and European whalers from faraway ports such as Nantucket, New Bedford, Sag Harbour, San Francisco, London and Le Havre were seeking Lord Howe Island's bounty and the brief sanctuary the Island offered.

The hunting of whales is believed to have commenced with the Basques; from their land bordering France and Spain as early as the 10th century and in the waters off Newfoundland 400 years later. However, it was not until the middle of the 16th century that official records were kept. Commercial whaling began in 1607 at Spitsbergen, an archipelago in the Arctic Ocean 650 km north of the Norwegian coast. European whalers quarrelled over the territory until 1618 when a compromise was reached – the Dutch limited their operations to North Spitsbergen and left the rest to the English, French and the German Hanseatic League.

With the decline of the English Muscovy Trading Company of London a few years later, the Dutch temporarily gained ascendancy in the lucrative whaling trade. In 1623 they established the port of Smeerenberg ('Blubber Town') on the west coast of Spitsbergen, for the purpose of 'flensing' (stripping and cutting) and boiling the blubber to extract the whale oil. However, the large profits from whaling continued only until about 1640 when the depletion of fish stocks forced the Dutch to venture further out into adjacent seas.

By the middle of the 17th century shore whaling had begun along the New England coast of America, where hunters pursued right whales (so named because they were slow moving and of moderate size – the 'right' whales to catch). Centres were first established on Long Island and Cape Cod before shifting to Nantucket and New Bedford. The latter eclipsed Nantucket as the whaling capital of the world in 1835 and remained in that position until about 1860.

The capture of a cachalot by a Nantucket sloop, blown out to sea in a gale in 1712, led to the discovery of the superior qualities of its oil; especially that from the cavity in its massive block-shaped head. Spermaceti, once used to manufacture fine candles, is clear high-quality oil that partially solidifies on exposure to air. Its resemblance to seminal fluid gave rise to the cachalot's common name – the sperm whale. As the value of this oil increased, ships were outfitted for longer voyages and pushed further into the ocean in pursuit of these whales. By 1775 they had sailed the Atlantic from the verge of the Arctic Circle to the west coast of South Africa, the east coast of South America, and as far south as the Faulkland Islands.

Disaster struck the Atlantic fishery with the American Revolution. Triggered by the British Navigation Acts that regulated commerce in England's interests, especially those of the East-India Company, tensions mounted between England and her American colonies from 1763. Trade restrictions and the imposition of various taxes saw a considerable reduction in exports from the colonies to England, and a boycott of English imports. The economic downturn resulted in extensive smuggling in the American carrying trade, which in turn led to arbitrary seizure of offshore shipping by the British navy.

By early 1775 war was imminent. With trade at a virtual standstill English whaleships, many captained by loyalist Americans, sailed around the Cape of Good Hope and established the British Southern Whale Fishery in the Indian Ocean. At first operations concentrated on southern black right whales which, like their northern cousins, could be taken from shore based stations as well as at sea. However, by the early 1800s these fish stocks had declined and, with an increasing demand for sperm oil, whalers began directing their operations to the Pacific where sperm whales were known to exist in great numbers.

Although the East-India Company forbade whaling east of the Cape of Good Hope, the American Revolution had weakened its power and eastbound activity increased annually. British convict ships, on their return to England, had already begun taking black whales along the eastern seaboard of Australia, and sperm whales on the continental shelf to the northwest. Within a few years, whalers from the Indian Ocean had entered the Pacific via the west coast of Australia, the Indonesian archipelago and Torres Strait.

Meanwhile, with the end of revolutionary hostilities, the newly formed United States of America floundered through a post-war depression. Industry, including the Atlantic Fishery, was at low ebb. Disrupted by years of naval warfare, whalers sought their fortunes elsewhere. In 1789, under licence from the East-India Company, the London whaling firm of Enderby & Sons sent the first British ship around Cape Horn, into the largest ocean in the world in pursuit of the sperm whale. Two years later the Americans followed – and the Pacific Whale Fishery was born.

Following the westward advance of the whales, American and British ships sailed via Galapagos along the Equator to the Gilbert and Ellice archipelago, then south into Australian and New Zealand waters. The profits were such that by 1801, the Enderby and Campion firms of London had secured further concessions from the East-India Company, which virtually threw the whole Pacific Ocean into free trade. By 1820 fifteen whaling grounds had been established. For three-quarters of a century a thousand ships fished the far reaches of the Pacific, provisioning at numerous islands within these grounds. And, as one of these ports, Lord Howe Island became part of whaling history.

Sailing on three and four year-long voyages whaleships had become seagoing factories, equipped with onboard brick tryworks to extract oil and store huge quantities for many years. It was an industry in which men sacrificed themselves to a life of unbelievable hardship on the open seas. Lashed by wind and rain, half frozen in Antarctic waters or baked in the tropics, they were also subjected to long hours of boredom as they waited weeks and sometimes months to sight their quarry. In 1851, Captain Samuel Braley of Massachusetts, wrote: -

> I don't know what has become of the whales: tis time they were on again…This whaling business is much like the Nantucket girls rolling down a sand hill and singing at every turn:
>
> Now you see it; now you don't
> Perhaps you will; perhaps you won't.

And, when the time came to hunt their elusive prey they were little more than tiny bobbing specks, in small oar-propelled boats on a vast ocean, engaging the largest

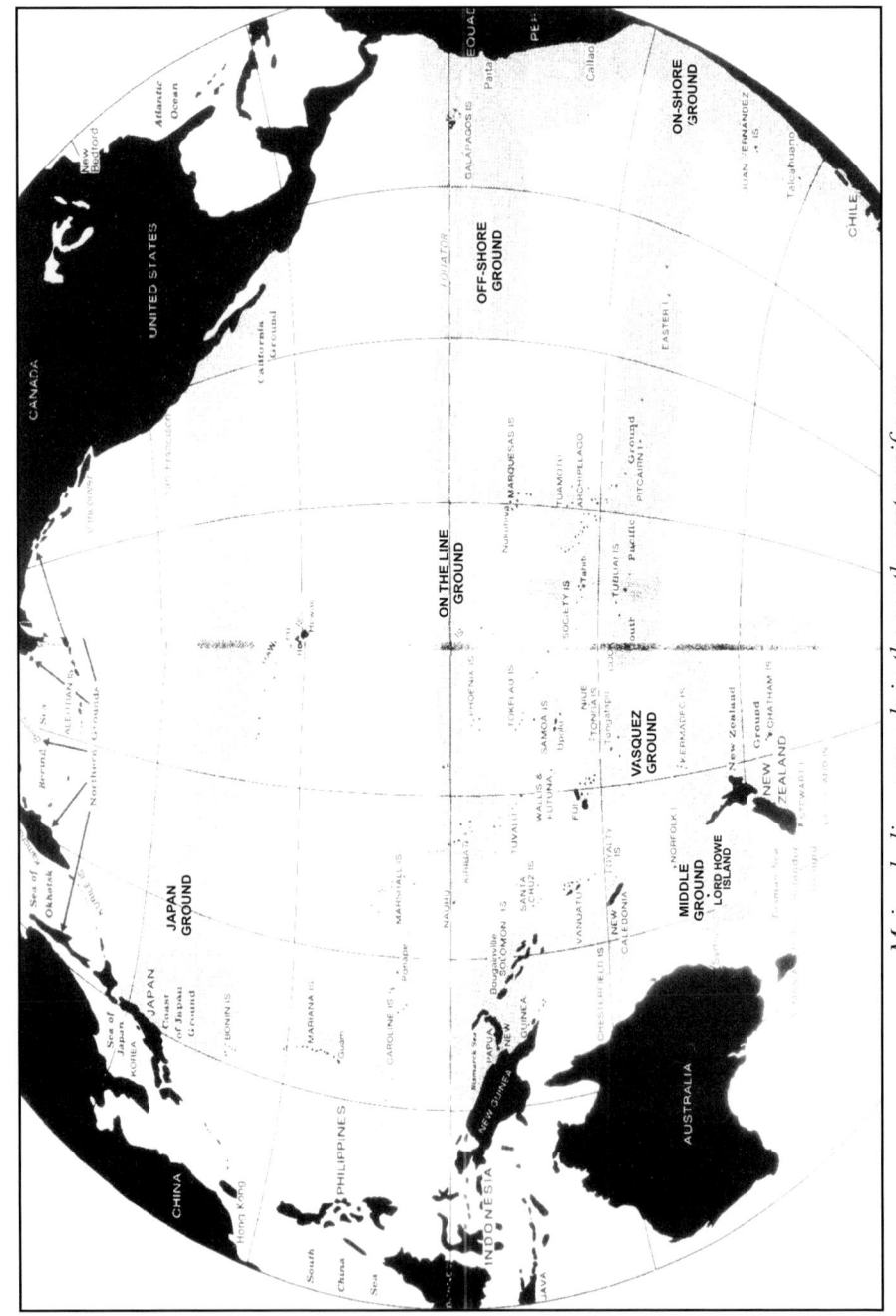

Main whaling grounds in the south-west pacific area
('The Whales Wake', H Morton, Dunedin, 1982)

22

mammals on earth with just hand-thrown harpoons and lances.

As Australia joined this international industry the prohibition against shipbuilding was raised, and by 1800 an established dockyard had launched the first two Australian ships. International whalers were also permitted to refit and take on provisions at Australian ports. The long voyages to and from the Pacific grounds even prompted some British vessels to transfer their registration from London to Sydney, or to use Sydney as a home port on a regular basis. English and American ships also engaged in double-cruising, which involved calling at various ports to transfer a complete cargo of oil to other trading vessels for shipment home. They would then head back to the whaling grounds for a second cargo before beginning the long voyage to their home ports.

Specific grounds were soon identified for sperm whales, and for southern black rights during their migration north from Antarctica. The Queensland coast to New Caledonia became the Northern Ground; Tasmania to Cape Leeuwin in Western Australia, the Western Ground; East of Tasmania to the Chatham Islands off New Zealand, the Eastern Ground; and between the New South Wales coast and northern New Zealand was known as the Middle Ground.

The Middle Ground, particularly the area between 29° to 35° south and 159° to 172° east, became one of the six major whaling grounds in the Pacific. The other five were: -

On-Shore – between the southern boundary of Chile and the northern limits of Peru; this ground extended to the southern coast of Ecuador and west to the Juan Fernandez and Galapagos Islands. (Sperm and right)

Off-Shore – an extension of the Onshore ground; it was identified between latitude 5° to 10° south, and longitude 90° to 120° west. (Sperm)

On-the-Line – this ground followed the equator from the coast of South America to the southern part of the Gilbert Islands (now Kiribati). (Sperm)

Japan – the east coast of Japan extending south to the Bonin Islands; between latitude 28° to 40° north and eastwards to longitude 170°. (Sperm)

Vasquez – from the seas around Fiji and Tonga; it connected with the Middle Ground. (Sperm, right and humpback)

With Lord Howe Island almost centre of the Middle Ground more than 200 ships, many from the 675-strong American fleet, laid anchor to provision over seven decades. The first recorded visit was by the American vessel *Ann and Hope* in 1798, but it was not until the 1830s that the industry prompted settlement and the establishment of a trading station.

According to Island records dating from 1839 and an index of places visited by American whalers in the Pacific, provided by the *Pacific Manuscripts Bureau*, the number of ships to make landfall until 1859 usually varied between five and twelve per year. However, the years 1842, 1843 and 1846 recorded 13, 18 and 17 visits respectively; and in 1855, 1856 and 1857 – 18, 17 and 21 visits were listed. It was during these periods that as many as seven or eight vessels, foul bottomed from years of cruising, lay off the reef at any one time. On 27 April 1858 the *Boston Daily Journal* reported in its whaling column: -

Touched at Lord Howe's Island Dec.7, barques *Elizabeth Swift* (Capt. Chase, New Bedford); 17th, *Sea Ranger* (Capt. Davis, Nantucket); *Menker* (Capt. Bloomfield, New Bedford); 28th, *Mohawk* (Capt. Grant, Nantucket); Jan.2, *Edward Carey* (Capt. Winslow, Nantucket) and *E.C. Cowdin* (Capt. Bailey, Dartmouth).

Food, water, wood and sand were sought. Pigs and goats were released to breed for the provision of fresh meat; and turtles were once again captured during the summer months. Tragically, two of the thirteen endemic species of landbirds and one seabird species identified in 1788 were hunted to extinction. A ground-dwelling bird known as the White Gallinule, the 'plump and good eating' White-throated Pigeon and the Tasman Booby, which nested along the lagoon foreshore, were the first to succumb to human impact.

Wood was needed to kindle fires under the ships' immense cauldrons or try-pots, and one tree in particular was favoured: -

a stunted tree found growing near the water, and which hums with a fierce heat

For many years it was known as 'whaler's wood' but Islanders today are unaware of the term, and can only hazard a guess as to what tree it referred to. The hotbark and berrywood have been suggested due to their size, burning capacity, and the areas in which they grow.

Whaling was a dangerous and messy business and the brutal slaughter of just one fish could take hours. Having fallen prey to the harpoon a whale fought a desperate battle, often ramming the open boats of its captors, until exhausted and the killing lance was used. Several attempts could be made before the weapon penetrated the group of coiled arteries, encased in a thick layer of blubber, in the vicinity of the lungs. Mortally wounded, death was not immediate and as the whale began to choke on its own blood – its spout, once a fountain of life – spewed a geyser of blood and gore. Only after final convulsions known as its 'flurry', would it finally succumb.

The whalers then began the enormous task of transforming their victim into the high-grade oil that illuminated the streets and lubricated the machines of the Industrial Age. Depending on its size, the entire operation could take two or three days. Towed by the whaleboats to the ship, the carcass was secured to the side where the flensing and boiling began. This process, known as 'trying-out', involved hacking a hole into the whale's side just behind the front fin. A giant 'blubber hook' suspended from the mast, and attached by ropes and chains to a system of pulleys, was then inserted into the hole. Operating from a lowered platform the men cut into the blubber which, pulled by the winch, was gradually stripped away. The blanket pieces were then severed from the whale and lowered into the blubber room where they were cut into smaller sections and boiled to render the oil.

As crispy pieces of blubber, known as 'scraps', floated to the surface of the pots they were skimmed off and tossed into the fire for fuel, thus limiting the need for extra wood during the trying-out process.

Once a sperm whale was completely stripped of blubber it was decapitated. The head accounts for close to a third of its length with the upper part containing the case; in which lies a reservoir of up to 526 gallons (2000 litres) of spermaceti. After the pulleys hauled the head up onto the deck, a large hole was cut in the case and buckets were used to remove the oil. Spillage was inevitable so if barrels of sand had been obtained while provisioning, it was scattered on the decks to prevent men from slipping in the mess of oil and blood. Before cutting loose a sperm whale's mutilated remains its intestinal tract was probed with a lance, in search of a black semiviscous and foul smelling liquid called ambergris. This fatty substance, thought to be the result of indigestion from a diet of cuttlefish, was valued for its supposed medicinal properties and as a fixative in perfume.

Only after the remains were finally discarded to feed other denizens of the deep, the oil stored in barrels and the ship scrubbed down, could whalers think of personal hygiene, which was difficult to maintain on whaleships at the best of times. Their skin and clothes were covered in a stinking mixture of oil, blood and smoke. Although bathing might have been a problem, laundry facilities were simple. A large tub placed in the break of the forecastle was used as a urinal. When it was full their trying-out clothes were soaked in the contents to remove the oil and blood before being rinsed in seawater.

Lord Howe Island's crystal clear lagoon and fresh water streams offered respite for whalers, worn and weary from their gruelling shipboard life.

The length of time whalers stayed at the Island depended largely on the amount of oil barrelled. If a ship was clean (no oil) it anchored only as long as it took to provision, before setting sail again. However, some ships several years out from their home ports and stored to capacity remained longer – perhaps rest and recreation for the crew before their long journey home.

On 26 February 1857 the names of the American barques *Belle*, *Rose* and *Mary Lake* and the names of some of their men were carved into a tree near Big Creek. By the 1970s the tree had succumbed to the ravages of weather and time, but part of the engraved bark is now displayed in the Island's Museum. The *Belle* was returning home with 2100 barrels of sperm oil. At about the same time *Wollaston* also provisioned. Nearly four years out of New Brunswick, she was returning with 1500 barrels of sperm oil and 1850 barrels of black oil.

Some whalers were called 'lucky ships' based on their success rate and the least number of disasters that befell them. The 320-ton *Belle* from Fairhaven and the 264-ton barque *Aladdin* from Hobart were two such ships.

The 31.5 m square stern *Belle*, built at Rochester in 1844, was a two deck, three masted vessel with billethead (the less expensive alternative to an elaborate figurehead), and no galleries (balconies projecting from the aft part of a ship's hull). She carried a complement of twenty-five men. Her first voyage to the Pacific Ocean began on 10 December 1844 and lasted nearly eight years, during which time she made landfall at Lord Howe Island on four occasions. Her next voyage from March 1853 to August 1857 brought *Belle* back to the Island on several provisioning stops. She made another long trip to the Pacific between October 1857 and May 1862 before being sold to foreign buyers in 1863.

Despite her impressive whaling career *Belle* met with some disasters. On one occasion she lost six of her crew, not to the sea but to warring Pacific natives – not Lord Howe Island's!

A 10-gun brig named *Mutine*, launched at Portsmouth, England in 1825, spent seventeen years as a warship before being sold to Bennet & Company, shipowners of London. Converted into a barque, her freeboard raised, and renamed *Aladdin,* she was sent whaling to the South Seas. When Bennett died in 1846 *Aladdin* was sold to Charles Seal, a shipowner in Tasmania. In what was considered a record for continual sailing, in 1868 she left Hobart and during her 17-month cruise of the whaling grounds, did not drop anchor once! *Aladdin* continued whaling until 1885 when the Tasmanian

Government purchased her then dismantled her for use as a coal hulk. Several years later she was converted into a storeship for gunpowder.

In her forty-three years as a whaler, records show that *Aladdin* courted disaster four times. In 1865 John Henry, the 6 year old son of her then master, Captain James McArthur, was killed when he fell down the ship's hold. He was buried in Pinetrees cemetery at Lord Howe Island. In February 1873 she ran aground at Ralphs Bay, Tasmania, and had to be lightened in order to refloat. In November 1880, another master, Captain Copping, died from head injuries received when a chain broke while trying-out a whale in the Solanders off the southern tip of New Zealand. The last incident, and perhaps one that the biblical Jonah would have envied, occurred in 1882 when one of her boat crew escaped from a bull whale that had charged open-mouthed and seized the bow. He fell into the gaping jaws of the whale but, through sheer luck or perhaps divine intevention, a large piece of wood from the boat's broken timbers prevented the jaws from closing on him, and he was pulled free.

Aladdin, like *Belle*, made many visits to Lord Howe Island and both ships brought with them men who would mark the beginning of two long bloodlines – the Nichols and Thompson families.

4

SETTLEMENT – AN INTRODUCTION

Courtesy of LHI Historical Society

Perry and Sarah Johnson's Thatched Cottage, 1882

Some islands are merely dreams of land in the mist of distant dreams. Lord Howe Island is such a place, a seven-mile long sliver in a strange and empty quarter of the sea. (David Doubilet, National Geographic)

By the 1830s, Lord Howe Island's recognition as a provisioning port had set the stage for future development and settlement commenced. Many descendants of the early settlers are residents today.

The Island beckoned and they came from far and wide – farmers, carpenters, seafarers, deserters and adventurers – in search of an Elysian lifestyle or wealth and prosperity. Several settlers were whaling captains. A special bond with the Island, formed during their years traversing the whaling grounds, drew them back. Some even continued their seafaring life, leaving their families to farm the land in their absence.

From trading farm produce to the cultivation and export of Lord Howe Island Red Onions and finally Kentia palm seeds, each industry met with success and failure. Self-reliance, determination and hard work were the core of Island enterprise, which probably shattered the Utopian myth for those settlers who stayed only a short time. However, by the turn of the century, the intelligent, rugged and sometimes feisty individuals who remained had created a small but multicultural society – insulated not only by distance but also by birthright.

These pioneers were squatters, but among themselves ownership of land was determined by the farms they established and any other improvements. Properties were generally bartered for as there was little or no money. Settlers departing would trade their holdings for passage off the Island or quantities of produce, such as potatoes and onions, that could be sold on the mainland. Properties changed hands on numerous occasions and today, while the sites occupied by the permanent settlers can be identified, many of those occupied by short-term residents are pure guesswork.

For more than forty years Lord Howe Island remained mostly a cashless society. Whalers preferred the Island trade to the harder bargains driven on the mainland. An array of farm produce along with goats, pigs, birds, timber and water were exchanged for stores of tea, sugar, salt, flour, soap, tools, clothing, tobacco and even quantities of American Medford Rum.

Many of the goods that the Islanders bartered for had travelled half way round the world. It was nothing to ask the captain of an American vessel to bring luxury items such as sewing machines or corn shellers on his next voyage, and then wait three years for delivery. Patience was indeed a virtue! As late as the mid twentieth century, some Island homes still contained New England furniture that had made the voyage around the Horn in the same hold as empty oil casks, beads, calico and other goods bound for trade in the South Seas.

In 1856 the American whaler *Louisiana* traded ploughs, other farming implements and a whaleboat for a ton of onions and a supply of arrowroot, coffee, sugar syrup, grapes, papaya, two casks of smoked muttonbirds, a bale of muttonbird feathers and six walking sticks! Returning to her home port of New Brunswick after more than four years at sea, it is unclear if the walking sticks were just souvenirs fashioned from the Island's timber or if they were needed by some of the ship's ageing crew!

An American influence lingered for many years. Apart from the visiting whalers one of the early settlers, also an American, brought many customs from his native town of Somerset in Massachusetts. Corned mush breakfasts, johnnycake, soda biscuits and slowly fried chicken rolled in flour became part of the Island's fare. Independence

Day was observed with the flying of the American flag and Thanksgiving was also celebrated.

When the Australian gold rushes began in 1851 the fear of men deserting ships for the gold fields caused captains to avoid the mainland and the Island trade increased, peaking between 1855 and 1857. Americans had already witnessed the damage desertion inflicted on the 'greasy luck' industry during the 1849 Californian gold rush, when whalers headed west to seek their fortunes in the earth as they had once sought in the sea.

However, the boom for the Island was not to last and times of hardship and isolation lay ahead. Whaling began a rapid decline from the early 1860s with the rise of the petroleum industry and the onset of the American Civil War. From 1860 to 1872 only forty-three ships provisioned; and from 1873 to 1887 less than a dozen. The last recorded visits by American whalers were *Palmetto* in 1881, *Robert Morrison* in 1882 and *John and Winthrop* in 1887. The last Australian ship to provision was the barque *Especulador* on 11 October 1881.

Captain H Poole of Dartmouth, USA when asked about his voyages to the Pacific, and if he knew Lord Howe Island, said: -

> My first visit to the island was in 1869 on the barque 'Minnesota'. The islanders exchanged fruit, vegetables and fowls for calico, flour, sugar, tea, tobacco, soap and shoes.
>
> My second visit was as master of the barque 'John and Winthrop' in 1887. 1430lbs. of Irish potatoes were bought for £6 per ton; 1278lbs. of sweet potatoes at £5 per ton; 700lbs. onions at £12 per ton; 51 bunches of bananas at 1/- or 1/6d. per bunch; 9 pairs of fowls at 30d. per pair and 413lbs. of beef at 3/6d. per pound. Tahiti oranges were not ripe but there were plenty of lemons, passion fruit and ripe corn.

In the wake of the declining whaling trade, the settlers relied heavily on the export of onions. However, by the early 1870s the crops were severely damaged by disease and that industry failed. This resulted in a dramatic decrease in visits by other trading vessels, after which the Islanders endured periods of six to eighteen months without even sighting a ship.

Commencement of the palm seed industry in the late 1870s promised a revival in trade with the mainland, but it was to be bittersweet. Its beginnings were of little benefit to the Islanders, bringing about a time of discontent and unrest. Later, a rat plague and two world wars would severely disrupt the industry. Nevertheless, it would eventually reemerge as a major enterprise on the Island, second only to tourism.

For many years the NSW Government paid little interest in the Island other than in its viability as a penal colony. Between various proposals and surveys, it was largely forgotten and the inhabitants were left to run their own affairs. That was until the diversity of its native flora and fauna, and in particular the Kentia palm, was found to be of immense scientific value. This enlightenment prompted a keener interest by the Government and ultimately its control of Island matters, including land tenure – a move that would generate a mistrust of mainland authority, which would pass down through generations of Island families, and still exists today.

5

FIRST SETTLERS – 1834-1848

Courtesy of LHI Historical Society

Group of Lord Howe Islanders, 1882

The vessel that carried the first settlers to Lord Howe Island in June 1834 sailed from the port of Russell, the capital of New Zealand at that time. The barque *Caroline,* commanded by Captain John Blinkenthorpe, landed three Englishmen at Ross Bay on the eastern side of the Island. The name of the bay was changed to Blinkenthorpe to reflect this landing, and is known today as Blinky Beach. It was believed the men had with them their Maori wives, two children and a brother of one of the women. However, an 1835 report on the tiny settlement suggests they could have come from a passing ship a short time later.

The Sydney merchant and whaling firm Robert Campbell & Co employed the three men, George Ashdown, James Bishop and Chapman (first name unknown) to establish a supply station for the flourishing whaling trade. They settled in huts at the western end of Hunter Bay, known now as Old Settlement, where they engaged in fishing and raising pigs and goats from feral stocks.

The first garden they cultivated was on an area west of Blinky Beach. A variety of produce, including potatoes, carrots, maize, pumpkin, taro and watermelon thrived in the fertile soil. Eventually they established gardens nearer Old Settlement where many years later, evidence of the cultivation of grapes, passionfruit and coffee still existed. The original Blinky Beach garden was covered by tonnes of material when the Island's airstrip was built in 1974.

Besides supplying passing ships with fresh vegetables, water, wood, fish and meat, the settlers ventured into the collection of muttonbird feathers. The feathers, used for bedding, were exchanged for clothing – referred to as 'slops' on whaling vessels. Hundreds of birds were slaughtered but the unpleasant smell of the feathers often made it difficult to trade them. James Bishop, an educated man, also acted as correspondent for the Sydney Monitor, a biweekly newspaper (1826-1841) and sent periodical lists detailing visiting ships.

The small population soon increased with George Ashdown and his partner, Emma (also known by the Maori name of Raukatauri), producing four children in as many years. Helena (Ellen) was born l4 October 1836, James David on 5 May l838, Sarah Louise on l7 July 1839, and Mareae on l7 December 1840.

In September 1841 the Island's potential as a whaling port caught the attention of Captain Owen Poole, a retired British officer from the Bombay Establishment. Arriving at the Island on the barque *Jane Elizabeth*, he bought out the settlers for £350 – Bishop and Chapman received £100 each and Ashdown received £150 on account of the greater improvements on his share of the land.

The party returned to New Zealand, although the exact dates are unknown. Ashdown certainly left soon after as his four children were christened at the Methodist Church in Manning Street, Wellington, on 14 November 1841. Chapman probably left about the same time, but Bishop's last recorded list of visiting ships sent to the Sydney Herald in 1843 suggests he departed that year.

What became of Chapman and Bishop is unknown. George Ashdown returned to whaling until 1845 when he joined the Militia in the first of the Maori wars. During the defence of the Otaka Pa he survived a horrific attack by Chief TeWhereWhere. He married twice more and eventually became a publican in Johnsonville, New Zealand, where he died in 1858. Little is known of his family except that his eldest daughter, Ellen, wed James Wilberforce in Victoria in 1857 and 136 years later their great-grandson, Graydon Hudspeth visited the Island.

Captain Poole (no relation to the American whaling captain previously mentioned) was in partnership with Richard Dawson from the firm Richard Dawson & Henry Augustus Castle, the first ironmongers in Sydney. Although there are no records of him having lived on the Island, the landmarks of Dawsons Peak, Dawsons Ridge, and Dawsons Point bear his name. A site almost immediately to the north of and overlooking Old Settlement, was named Pooles Lookout.

Upon purchasing the business, the following advertisement was placed in the *Sydney Herald* on 13 September 1841: -

IMPORTANT TO SHIPPING

Notice is hereby given that a station and store is formed at Lord Howe's Island situated in Latitude 31° 36′ South, and Longitude 159°04′ East, where whaling and other vessels can be provided with livestock, Fish, Potatoes and other Vegetables, Slops, etc., on moderate terms.

Vessels approaching the Island can be communicated with by a Boat, which is kept for the purpose of conveying supplies; consequently Masters will not find it requisite for any of their men to leave the ship. The Settlement is on the West side of the Island.

The same notice appeared in 1842 in the *Morning Register*, New Bedford on 25 May; the *Nile's National Register*, Baltimore on 4 June; the *Daily Advertiser*, Boston on 6 June; and the *Boston Semi-Weekly Advertiser* on 8 June.

The first people employed to work the station in December 1841 were Messrs Wright, Hescott, McAuliffe and their wives. Wright had been Master on the *Jane Elizabeth* that had brought Captain Poole to the Island. Hescott had previously visited in 1839 as Captain on the small cutter *Rover's Bride*. Although a corruption of his name, Erscotts Passage and Erscotts Hole were named after Hescott.

Rover's Bride became the first regular trading vessel to operate between Sydney and the New Hebrides via Lord Howe Island. Between 1842 and 1852 she proved a reliable link and when the onion industry was established, she was used for their export. Unfortunately, while trading in sandalwood in the New Hebrides in December 1852, she was lost off the coast of the island of Erromanga

Captain Middleton and his wife, Eliza, arrived as independent settlers in 1841, making their home at Callam Bay. Their hut was situated on an area now known as The Cut Grass Patch where they farmed, raised pigs and were noted for digging the Island's first well. They left the Island in 1855. It is unknown if Finger Peak was named by Lieutenant Ball or by whalers, but Captain Middleton renamed it Mount Eliza after his wife. Callam Bay is known today as North Bay.

In July 1842 Poole and Dawson engaged Thomas and Margaret Andrews as servants for one year. They left after the year, but their return for another term of employment in 1844 would mark the beginning of a long line of descendants on the Island.

In 1843 Alan Isaac Mosely and his wife, Johanna, commenced a long period of residency. They too worked for Poole and Dawson. Known as Isaac, he was from England and was the navigating officer on the whaler *Jane*. After meeting and falling in love with Johanna, he smuggled her on board in a whale oil barrel liberally provided with air holes. When the Master of the vessel discovered her several days after leaving Sydney, he decided she should be put ashore at the nearest land – Lord Howe Island.

After completing that voyage, Isaac left the ship to join his sweetheart. Their marriage ceremony, conducted by Captain Poole, was the first on the Island. However, nearly fifty years later on being told the ceremony was illegal, they were officially married on 3 June 1892 by W E Langley, the Island's Registrar of Births, Deaths & Marriages.

In July 1844 Dr John Foulis bought half of Poole's interest. He arrived on the passenger schooner *Wave* with his wife, daughter, and four young Englishmen – Platter, Slade, Thorne and Varney. The men were employed to work for him for £10 each per annum plus single ration. During the landing, one of the boats belonging to the settlement was dashed to pieces against rocks and three crewmen of the *Wave* lost their lives. The first body recovered, believed to be a man named Ned, was buried in the sands of the bay where the accident occurred. The bodies of John Duncan and James Sanson were recovered two days later and buried alongside him.

Neds Beach was reputedly named after this incident although many of the older Islanders disputed it claiming it was named after the ex-whaler Ned Ambrim, who had a garden in that area.

Dr Foulis established a farm to the north of Windy Ridge (Windy Point). By all accounts, he was a rather eccentric person who always wore a long brown coat that resembled the colour of a now extinct bird – the Ouzel or Vinous tinted Blackbird, then locally known as the Doctor Bird.

The Andrews also returned to the Island on the *Wave* and after completing their second term as servants for Captain Poole, they moved to an area at the southern end of the Island that they named Big Creek. There they went into partnership with Wright and Mosely, farming about 44 acres of land. Their only child, Mary, was born on 31 December 1846.

In 1847, after failing to obtain a lease on their holdings from the New South Wales Government, Poole and Foulis abandoned the settlement. Their remaining employees,

Hescott, McAuliffe and the four Englishmen, were given the choice of returning to Sydney or continuing on the Island as independent settlers. They chose to leave.

Captain Poole gave his holdings at Old Settlement to the Andrews to use as they wished. Dr Foulis, in exchange for passage to Sydney on the American whaler *General Pike,* transferred his holdings to Captain Pierce, the master of that ship. Foulis left with his family, which by then included a 2 year-old son, on 9 August 1847.

In 1848 Captain Pierce decided to return to sea and transferred his property to the Andrews in exchange for two tons of potatoes. By mutual agreement, the partnership between Andrews, Wright and Mosely was dissolved. Wright continued the farm alone, moving into the Andrews' original home south of Big Creek. By that time he and his wife had two daughters, Anne and Jane, born in 1842 and 1844 respectively. The family remained on the Island until 1864.

Isaac and Johanna established their own farm on an area between Blinky Beach and Prince William Henry Bay or 'Two Mile Beach', known today as the Lagoon. They remained at Mosely Park for the rest of their lives but had no children. Isaac died on 1 June 1897 aged 87, after 54 years residency. Johanna died 14 May 1911 aged 97, after 68 years residency. At the time of her death, Johanna still had the whale oil barrel that was used to smuggle her on board the *Jane* so many years before.

With substantial holdings at Old Settlement and Windy Point, the Andrews' farming activities increased to include the cultivation of onions. Margaret began this industry in 1848 after finding some on the beach, presumably thrown overboard from a passing vessel. For nearly thirty years the Lord Howe Island Red Onion, famous for its keeping qualities, was sought after throughout the Southern Hemisphere. With a yearly production rate of over 30 tons these onions occupied nine-tenths of the land under cultivation, until the prevalence of smut severely damaged the industry.

Shortly before his death in 1860 Thomas Andrews introduced oranges from Tahiti, the pips having been planted in boxes on board the American whaler *Napoleon*. This marked the beginning of citrus cultivation on the Island.

By 1849 Lord Howe Island was home to just eleven people, two of whom were the progenitors of an Island dynasty. Within a few years more settlers would follow and as the Island farms expanded, there was no shortage of extra hands to help work the land. Whalers eager to leave a life of stove ships, scurvy and other hardships at sea, traded their existence for paradise – some for only a short time, while others remained for many years.

AN ARCHAEOLOGICAL FIND

On 26 October 2004, 170 years after the arrival of Ashdown, Bishop and Chapman, an archaeological excavation unearthed the foundations of what is believed to be the house of George Ashdown. Kimberley Owens, a PhD candidate from the Department of Archaeology and natural History, and her colleagues, undertook the work for the Research School of Pacific and Asian Studies at the Australian National University in Canberra.

Using ground mapping radar they located the historic find, buried approximately a metre deep, on a mound close to the shoreline at the northern end of Old Settlement. The remains, measuring about 6 by 4 metres, had a base made of orb-shaped basalt rocks of the kind found on several Island beaches, and was covered by a clay floor. Indications were that the walls were made of palm thatch panels with two tree trunks, probably from the Island's palms, supporting a pitched thatch roof. A nearby mound, having similar foundations beneath it, is believed to be another of the original sites recorded in 1835. This site was not excavated. However, animal bone fragments, artefacts and other materials taken from the dig provided a valuable insight into the lives of the first settlers on Lord Howe Island.

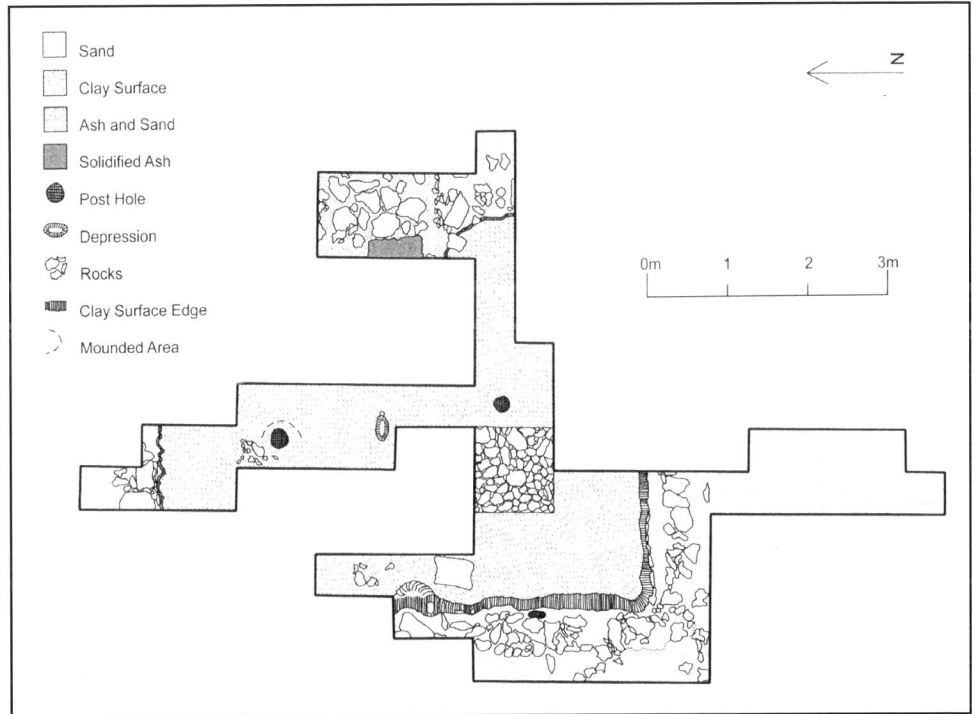

Plan of hut foundation excavated at Hunter Bay

6

A PENAL COLONY – TO BE OR NOT TO BE!

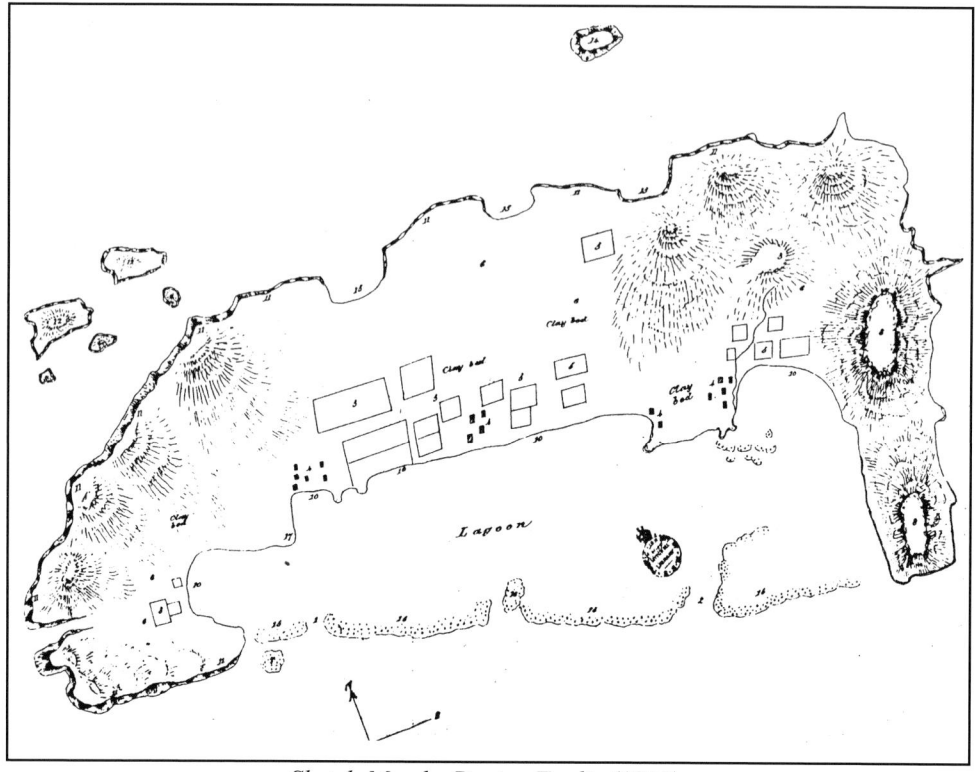

Sketch Map by Doctor Foulis (1851)

For thirty-five years, the future of the little community was threatened as the Government entertained several proposals to establish a penal colony on Lord Howe Island.

During the tenure of Ashdown, Bishop and Chapman, an escaped convict from Hobart, William Powis, and two crew members from the schooner *Adelaide,* who had aided and abetted his escape, were put ashore on the Island. On hearing of the incident the authorities in Sydney despatched the revenue cutter *Prince George*, commanded by Captain Roach (the largest of the Admiralty Islands so named), to pick up the offenders and return them to Sydney.

The Government took advantage of the visit to obtain a survey on the suitability of the Island as a penal settlement. H J White, Assistant Surveyor of Sydney, was appointed to conduct the survey.

On 18 December 1834, the Sydney Gazette printed the following: -

The expedition to Howe's Island, for the purpose of reporting on the practicability of devoting it to the purposes of an enlarged prison, upon the principle of Norfolk Island, is the first indication of the promised abandonment of Moreton Bay, a place where facilities to escape are numerous, and when the ague and other afflictions and diseases prevail to a fearful extent. To be perfect a penal settlement for the reception of double convicted, and desperate offenders must be wholly destitute of every possible incentive for the convict to put restraint and discipline at defiance, and to encounter the hazard of the wild bush and savages, in the desperate hope of avoiding the affliction of one evil for others of less possible occurrence. In this respect, Howe's Island will be preferable to Moreton Bay.

White, in his report of January 1835, concluded that the Island was unsuitable for such a colony. He cited the lack of anchorage in the harbour (Prince William Henry Bay) for ships of more than 30 or 40 tons, the scarcity of fresh water in the lowland area and the poor soil seemingly unfit for growing wheat. Attached to his report was a map showing the settlers' huts towards the western end of Hunter Bay and the garden near Blinkenthorpe Bay. Of the inhabitants he wrote: -

There were three white men (English) on the island, and each of them had a wife and a numerous family; their wives were New Zealand women, which they had picked up, somehow or other, from ships putting in for food. Those three Robinson Crusoes, a big lad, brother to one of the women, and their families, constituted the whole of the population. They had plenty of pigs, goats, poultry, and dogs for hunting; besides a canoe for catching fish, so they did not want any provisions, whatsoever may have been their other privations. We saw growing pumpkin, watermelon, potatoes, onions, cabbages, and other vegetables, all of which were cultivated with care, and appeared in a healthy condition

After his report was tabled, the establishment of a penal colony on the Island was forgotten for another sixteen years and the settlers were left alone to continue their agricultural pursuits.

Between 1851 and 1853, as a result of an anti-transportation movement on the mainland, the Island once again attracted the attention of the Government as a possible penal colony.

The dumping grounds for British criminals, bankrupts and other undesirables began with settlements at Port Jackson and Norfolk Island in 1788; later extending to other territories under the dependency of New South Wales. However, as the 19th century progressed, Australia began developing rapidly. The introduction of wheat and sheep farming formed the basis of the economy and systematic permanent colonisation began replacing the old penal settlements. As the territories separated from New South Wales between 1825 and 1863, there was growing opposition to the deportation of convicts from Britain.

Transportation to New South Wales temporarily ceased in 1841, leaving Van Diemens Land (separated in 1825) the only colony at that time to continue receiving convicts.

Britain's attempt to revive transportation was met with resistance from powerful associations within the new colonies. So intense was the opposition that when the ship *Hashemy* arrived in Sydney in 1849, an angry demonstration ensured it would be the last convict shipment to New South Wales.

The resistance movement united as a single organisation on 1 January 1851. Known as the Australasian League, it was successful in ending deportation of convicts to Australian shores. That same year, the League was also ultimately responsible for the granting of a new Constitution conceding self-government to the free colonies of New South Wales, Victoria, Van Diemens Land, South Australia and Western Australia. However, the Act under which Van Diemens Land gained its complete independence and became Tasmania was not brought into force until 1856.

For a time it appeared the efforts of the Australasian League would adversely affect the Island community. The difficulty of finding a place sufficiently isolated for the detention of criminals of the worst class from New South Wales and Victoria, directed attention to Lord Howe Island. In 1851 the New South Wales Government asked Dr Foulis, as a former Island resident, to submit a report on its suitability as a penal settlement. Extracts from his report dated 1 September 1851, which included a diagram of the Island showing improvements thereon, stated: -

> Howe's Island has for many years been a place of resort for whalers to procure wood, water, and fresh provisions, to enable them to prosecute their voyage without the necessity of going into Port.

> I believe there are at present, about 16 persons residing on the island, some of them having their wives and families and they enjoy uninterrupted good health.

> The settlers all have gardens and huts, which they have built of the cabbage tree. They live by trading with whalers, catching pigs and fish, and growing vegetables and fruits.

> The Mutton Bird (which serves as an article of food, and is much esteemed by the inhabitants), visits the island at certain seasons in flocks of thousands to lay its eggs in the ground, at which time it is caught in great numbers for the sake of its feathers.

It is only the young unfledged birds that are eaten, as they are free from any fishy rankness.

There are no snakes, rats, mice, native cats, nor other wild animals, except pigs and goats.

I should consider the island sufficiently large and fertile to support a population of 5,000, if under proper control, and capable of supplying them with all necessaries of life. Some coal may be required after a time, though for some years there would be an abundance of firewood. 60 to 80 whaling vessels per year have called here for provisions, and it has often happened that we have had English news from American ships some time before same was known in the main colony. The big hills are inaccessible cliffs about 4,000 feet high.

Following Dr Foulis' report, which exaggerated the heights of the mountains and the number of visiting whaling vessels, the Government favourably considered the proposed penal colony. However, the idea was abandoned after a meeting of the Executive Council, held on 17 February 1852, decided that the 526 prisoners to be relocated was too small a number, compared to the cost of maintaining a prison establishment on Lord Howe Island. The Council recommended that New South Wales enter into an arrangement with Van Diemens Land for the relocation and maintenance of prisoners to the penal colony on Norfolk Island.

Norfolk Island had been a prison settlement from 1788 until 1813 when the flax and timber venture failed. The settlement was disbanded in 1814 and all the buildings were burned or demolished to deter occupation by the French, who were Britain's main competitor in the Pacific. However, in 1825, Captain Richard Turton reoccupied Norfolk Island as a settlement for the worst felons from New South Wales. It would then remain a penal colony for the next thirty years. When transportation first ceased to New South Wales in 1841, Norfolk Island was annexed to Van Diemens Land.

The Executive Council's recommendation for the relocation of prisoners to Norfolk was rejected by Sir William Denison, Governor of Van Diemens Land, who was planning to reduce the number of convicts already on Norfolk. Finally, in January 1853, because of its isolation and disciplinary problems, it was decided to close the colony altogether, and permit occupation of the Island by 194 descendants of the Bounty mutineers living on Pitcairn Island.

The Council was once again asked to consider Lord Howe Island as a penal settlement. Captain Henry Denham of HMS *Herald*, at the request of Sir Charles A. Fitzroy, Governor-General of the Australian Colonies, explored the possibility while carrying out the first hydrographic survey of the island in July 1853. His report, a lengthy detailed document giving a favourable account and strongly recommending the Island's utilisation as a penal settlement, was referred to the Colonial Secretary. However, Denham's endorsement of their home as a prison would not have sat well with the Islanders of whom he wrote: -

> It appears that during the last ten years, Andrews, Mosely and Wright have by tacit permission, without rent or acknowledgment, cultivated with most commendable industry several plots of cleared land, which are delineated in outline upon the chart which accompanies this report.

> These people, with their serving men and children, comprising a little community of sixteen persons, not only derive a comfortable subsistence but store up the surplus of their crops for whalers and other vessels who may accidentally or intentionally approach the island and require refreshments. The supplies in question are of a sort very much to be desired by a whaler or a chance passenger vessel driven to the northward and eastward out of her path to Sydney, and consist of pigs, poultry, potatoes, and every variety of fruit and vegetable, not omitting that indigenous esculent the palm cabbage nor the fish which abound.

On 24 October 1853 the Executive Council decided that Denham's findings should be put to Parliament, with a recommendation that a Select Committee be appointed to report on the expediency of forming a penal settlement at the Island for the colonies of New South Wales, Victoria and South Australia. Fortunately, it was never tabled and yet again, the matter was temporarily forgotten.

Following an 1869 police investigation into the death of a whaler the Government, still pondering the prison question, once again considered utilising the Island as a penal colony.

Water Police Magistrate P J Cloete informed the Government that Surveyor White's report of 1835 was accurate; except for alleging that fresh water was scarce in the lowland area, when in fact *it was most abundant and excellent in quality*. The contradiction could have been because White's visit was in the dry summer period, while Cloete's visit took place in the wet winter season. His comments were duly noted and a Government pamphlet concluded with the following recommendation: -

> Lord Howe Island, from its position, climate, and capabilities, would be most suitable for a penal settlement; not particularly adapted for the management of desperate criminals, who might find means, however dangerous, to escape occasionally, but for that class where alienation from their homes, and isolation from their friends, would be a far greater punishment than other degradations which have now occasionally to be resorted to

Although strong arguments persisted in favour of a penal settlement, citing the relatively low costs compared to the upkeep of mainland establishments, the proposal was finally rejected and the matter laid to rest forever.

Seabirds of Lord Howe Island

7

THE PERMANENT SETTLERS

Nathan Thompson, Jack Brian and George Campbell arrived at Lord Howe Island early in 1853 on the American barque *Belle*. With them were two women, Boranga and Bogaroo, and a young girl, Bokue, all from Abemama in the Gilbert Islands. The party claimed a substantial area between Neds Beach and Thompsons Point, known today as Signal Point or Flagstaff. They also established a farm at the south end of the Island. In the forty-two years until his death, Nathan farmed and piloted visiting vessels to safe harbour. He was also the accepted mediator in any community disputes in the simple politics of the early days.

Jack Brian left on HMS *Herald* in July 1853. George Campbell died on the Island in 1856. Of the women, Bogaroo remained single and her death in December 1880 was the first officially recorded death on the Island. Nathan took Boranga as his partner, but she died in 1864 shortly after the death of their 11 year-old son, Hugh. By then Bokue was about 25 years old and she became Nathan's second partner. Their union produced three boys (one died in infancy) and three girls. Many of their descendants live on the Island today.

Michael Thompson, one of Nathan's great-grandsons, now owns the original Thompson home, Sunnyside. The first timber dwelling, it was built of planks sawn from local trees and cedar drift logs from a wrecked ship. It is situated opposite Thompson's Store which, as the Island's first general store, was established in 1927 by Nathan's eldest son, William.

On 2 May 1854 the Governor of NSW, Sir Charles A Fitzroy, arrived on HMS *Calliope* on what was to be the first vice-regal visit to the Island. Unfortunately, the weather conditions were gale force and the official party was unable to land. However, on 4 May the ship's chaplain, Reverend Carwithen, braved the high seas to take a Union Jack ashore and on that day performed the first baptisms on the island. The children christened were: -

Mary Andrews, Hugh Thompson, Anne and Jane Wright

Eight years later, in July 1862, Captain Tom Nichols arrived from Hobart on the barque *Aladdin*. He fell in love with Mary Andrews, not yet 16 years of age, and less than a month later he took her to Norfolk Island where they were married on 10 August. They made their home on the Andrews' property but Tom continued whaling for many years. However, his return to home port generally signalled another pregnancy. In the next twenty-two years the marriage produced eleven children – six daughters and five sons, two of whom died in infancy.

The Nichols family, 1897

Back: William Nichols, Martha Nichols, Norton Farnell (behind with hat), Mary Nichols, Hector Innes, Edith Kirby,
George Waterhouse (behind with hat), Tom Nichols
Middle: Robert Thompson, Gwendolyne Nichols (nee Garth), George Nichols, Grace Innes (nee Nichols),
Grandma Nichols (holding Tom Innes), Amelia Nichols (nee Griffiths) (holding Osborne Nichols), Charles Nichols
Front: Susan Nichols, Anne Nichols

45

A portion of land near Middle Beach that Tom eventually cleared for grazing cattle, became known as Nichols Clear Place. Mary Nichols' name was later given to a prominent boulder directly below the Black Face on Mount Lidgbird. It was dubbed Mother Nichols Rock after she once sought overnight shelter under the boulder.

William Nichols, a former gold prospector and the younger half-brother of Tom, also arrived on the *Aladdin*. He settled at North Bay where evidence of his garden remained for many years. Like most other homes on the Island, his was built of palm leaves and split palm battens but he was the first to use calico lining, which was dipped into a lime solution to whiten and stiffen it. He then commenced exporting lime which he manufactured by crushing and burning coral from the reef. He also exported bèche-de-mers and fungus found on the palms to China; and native seeds and spores to the mainland.

William married Hannah Baker in 1872. Of their twelve children, the first six died in infancy. Hannah hated living at North Bay as it was too far from the social scene. After their house and garden were completely destroyed in a severe storm in 1881, Mary Nichols transferred her land at Old Settlement (willed to her by her mother) to William and Hannah. There they established gardens, including a pine grove, adjacent to Old Settlement Creek. They also operated a small shop in their new home that was built east of the creek.

Sixty-five years later their grandson, Eric Hines, opened the Curio Shop on the same site. After Eric's death in 1963 the property changed hands several times, and today is the tourist resort Arajilla Retreat. Eric's sister, Ilma Sainsbury, recently passed away having lived for many years on a property that was once part of her grandfather's land.

In 1864 Charles Thorngrave and 18 year-old Edward 'Ned' King, both from England, arrived on the schooner *Gleaner* on which Ned had been employed as a cook. They settled an area near Middle Beach, which today is a Special Lease held by Ned's grandson, Les King. Thorngrave remained on the Island only a short time but Ned acquired the Wright farm upon that family's departure. He later acted as a mountain guide for survey expeditions; and was credited as the first person to climb both Mount Gower and Mount Lidgbird. Ned is also considered to have been the first exporter of Kentia palm seeds. His marriage to Janet Clarke produced six children, including two sets of twins. The eldest daughter died as the result of a childhood accident. The original home known as Janetville is today owned by another grandson, Gower Wilson, and members of his family.

Several landmarks were named after Ned including Kings Beach (near Salmon Beach) and Old Kings Cave (or Neds Cave) – a series of caves or overhangs at the foot of the cliffs on the northern ridge of Mount Gower.

In May 1869 the NSW Government conducted a scientific survey of the Island. The staff of observation included three representatives from the Botanic Gardens, Surveyor R.D. Fitzgerald, who was a Collector for the Australian Museum, and Tombone, an aboriginal tracker also known as Shoalhaven Billy.

Surveyor Fitzgerald, who befriended the Islanders, wrote in his report: -

> The inhabitants are, with two or three exceptions Europeans or Americans who have for the most part, been connected with the whaling trade; of a class quite equal, in my opinion, to the settlers on land in Australia, and are thirty-five in number. They seem to be very fairly provided with the necessities of life, but to lack money, as their trade with the whalers is, in great part, carried on by barter. They exchange pork, potatoes, maize, fowls and onions for tea, sugar, clothes, etc., which must be taken at the whalers' valuation.

> The houses are well built of split palm battens, thatched on the roof and sides with palm leaves. The leaf hangs down and the stem is bent over one horizontal batten and outside the next lower, an arrangement which gives a very white, clean appearance to the inside, somewhat resembling basket work, and very distinct from any other style of building. Each house is surrounded by outhouses, the sides of which are sometimes not thatched, and have a very light tropical appearance. They consist of barns, fowlhouses, houses for goats, pigs and dogs and drying floors for onions. Each house with its surrounding buildings, encircled by a fence of split palms and backed by lemon trees, arching banyans and clustering palm trees, is a picture of tropical comfort and beauty – not often to be seen or easily forgotten. The tillage is performed principally by hand labour, as there are only two horses on the island.

By 1871 the little community had produced more children. On 11 September that year HMS *Rosario,* returning to Sydney from official duties at Elizabeth Reef, anchored off Lord Howe Island. There was still no resident clergyman so at the request of the inhabitants, Commander Henry G Challis went ashore to conduct the baptism of eight children, including three of Thomas and Mary Nichols and four of Nathan and Bokue Thompson: -

Albert William Stanley Nichols
Charles Henry Osborn Nichols
Mary Challis Nichols
Mary Thompson
William Osborn Spurling Thompson
Emeline Thompson
Rosario Thompson
Harry Wainwright

Harry Wainwright was the child of a family addressed in Chapter 8. Mary Nichols was given her second name after the ship's Commander, and Rosario was named after the ship.

Albert, Charles and William were given names after Captain William Osborn Spurling (see Chapter 9). George Nichols was two years old at the time, but his name does not appear on the baptismal list.

The small ketch *Comet* began trading in 1873. Built in 1843 she was owned by Messrs Parsonage & Baker who, rather than run the vessel for profit, intended her to benefit the Islanders after the loss of the *Sylph* (see chapter 8). However, too much money was lost and the scheme eventually failed. In 1876, after laying at anchor for several months in what is now known as Comets Hole, she was taken back to Sydney and sold. Captain Baker's daughter, Hannah, became the wife of William Nichols.

In March 1876 HMS *Pearl* heralded her arrival with all the pomp and splendour of naval fanfare, much to the delight of the Islanders. While at anchor Grace Marguerite Pearl Nichols, second daughter of Tom and Mary, was christened by the ship's chaplain and given her second name in honour of the ship.

As the Andrews' farms flourished so did their acquisition of land. Thomas died in 1860 but by 1878 Margaret's holdings encompassed land from what is now T C Douglass Drive to the fuel storage site near the airport; as well as most of the cleared land at Old Settlement. That year she willed all her land and property in a Deed of Gift to her daughter Mary Nichols.

As Tom and Mary's children married and 'left home', land was apportioned to each of them. Edith, Mary's favourite daughter, would eventually acquire the family homestead on the original Foulis property. Built around 1884, it was known as Captain Nichols' Homestead and later The Pines. The property has since passed down through Edith's family. Today Pinetrees is owned by her granddaughters Kerry McFadyen, Pixie Rourke, and their husbands.

Thomas Bryant Wilson arrived on the Island in October 1878. Known as T B, he was born in England in 1843 and, after a sound education, enlisted in the military in 1860. He served as one of Princess Alexandra's bodyguards in 1863, at the time of her marriage to the Prince of Wales in Denmark. Later, as a soldier in Her Majesty's 14th Regiment, he fought in the Maori Wars in New Zealand. After T B retired from military service, he was employed as overseer in the Thames Mining Company near Auckland until early 1878. He then spent some months on Norfolk Island before embarking on a journey to visit his mother, Sarah, in Suffolk. However, he did not complete the journey.

On arriving at Lord Howe Island, T B met Captain Armstrong, the Government appointed Forest Ranger and Registrar of Births, Deaths & Marriages (see chapter 12). When Captain Armstrong learned that T B had served in the military under his brother, he invited him

48

ashore. A strong friendship developed and Armstrong persuaded T B to remain on the Island as a teacher. Some children were already in their teens and had received no formal education. On 29 July 1879 he was officially appointed the Island's first schoolmaster.

T B resigned in May 1880, possibly because he was having an affair with one of his students, and returned to New Zealand. However, he stayed there only a short time before returning to marry his sweetheart on 2 December 1880. Mary Thompson, the eldest child of Nathan and Bokue, was twenty-one years his junior but the union was a long and happy one, producing three sons and three daughters whose descendants form a large proportion of the population today. Larhonette, the home of their grandson Larry Wilson, is built on the site of the original family home, opposite the jetty area.

T B's interests were many and varied. He instructed Island women in midwifery; and from 1916 to 1920, he served the Church of England as a devoted worker and lay preacher. A keen gardener, he was responsible for propagating Norfolk Island pines from seeds he had intended to take back to England. He also saw the potential for exporting the Kentia palm seed and sent small parcels to his sister in England, a nursery contact in America, and the Curator of Kew Gardens in London.

He loved poetry and filled notebooks with his favourites by Shelley, Byron and Browning. A journal containing his own verse from 1876 to 1878 was found by Larry when he rebuilt his home in the 1970s. T B also kept a diary that covered almost fifty years of his life on the Island.

The first official record of birth on Lord Howe Island was that of Edith Nichols, third daughter of Tom and Mary, born on 2 November 1879. Shortly after, the mission steamer *Dayspring* visited the Island. Reverends Copeland and Laurie held a service and christened Edith and John Maxwell Thompson, second son of Nathan and Bokue. Two visitors, Mr & Mrs McKee, en route to Noumea on the ketch *Collingwood*, attended the service. They had visited the Island several times and befriended the inhabitants. Infant John was named after John Maxwell McKee.

John Robbins arrived on the schooner *Ephemey* in February 1880 and, after a short courtship, married Mary Mooney on 4 April that year. They lived in Mary's house for a time before settling at the south end of the Island. Of their four children, two died in infancy. Ysobel Heffernan, a granddaughter of John and Mary, lives on the Island today. (The Mooney family is addressed in chapter 9.)

Daniel Hamill settled in 1888 and soon married Rosario Thompson, youngest daughter of Nathan and Bokue. They had two children. Their son, William, lost his life at sea in 1936. The marriage did not last and mystery still surrounds the fate of Daniel. For years rumours persisted that he had drowned off Blinky Beach but most of the older Islanders believed he simply tired of Island life, boarded a departing vessel and vanished. Rosario wed again in 1906 and descendants from both marriages reside on the Island today.

Phillip Dignam and his cousin, Harry Payten, first visited the Island on a whaler. They were both 17 years old when they returned to work for Isaac Mosely in 1890. Before long Phillip was offered a partnership in the farm and built a home on Mosely's land. However, in 1891 he was given a chance to buy his own farm. With Isaac's blessing and much assistance from Islanders, his house was moved to its new site just north of T C Douglass Drive. This road was once the borderline between the properties held by Phillip Dignam and Mary Nichols. Harry, who later co-founded the Island's Bowling Club, worked for Phillip and after the business was established, they were joined by other family members from Goulburn.

In 1896 Phillip's widowed father, William, arrived with his three other children – Arthur, Jim and Lena. Arthur was only 6 years old and after schooling on the Island then at Hawkesbury College, he began working on a farm in Mudgee, NSW. At the outbreak of World War 1 he joined the A.I.F. and lost his life in France in 1916.

Jim also attended Hawkesbury College before finding employment on the mainland. After returning to the Island in the early 1930s he married Eileen Heffernan, daughter of the resident Church of England minister. They had three children – Jill, Joan and Dymity. The girls completed their education at a private college and remained on the mainland. Jim and Eileen died in 1968 within a week of each other. Today Peter and Judy Riddle (daughter of Roy and Daphne Wilson) live on the site of the Dignam property at the top of McGees Parade. Their house overlooks a point near Middle Beach, bearing Jim's name.

In 1897 Lena married William Thompson, first son of Nathan and Bokue. They had eleven children. The youngest died in infancy and William and Lena would outlive four other children, including a son who died in World War II.

Phillip's marriage in 1898 to Emeline Thompson, second daughter of Nathan and Bokue, produced four daughters and a son. Two daughters died in childhood. Besides farming, Phillip became Island agent for the Burns Philp Steamship Company and the Vacuum Oil Company. The latter, based at Balmain docks in Sydney, was eventually taken over by Mobil Oil. His son Phillip jnr would later carry on the agencies. Phillip maintained a long friendship with his former employer Isaac Mosely. Shortly before his death in 1897, Isaac willed his holdings to Phillip on the condition that he look after Johanna. Phillip complied with those wishes and after Isaac's death he cared for Johanna for another fourteen years. Phillip's property, known as Thornleigh, is today owned by his granddaughter Patricia Dignam. The original Mosely holdings form part of her Special Lease.

William Retmock, a sea captain, was believed to have been born Wilhelm Retzloff in Germany and upon settling in Australia he anglicized his name. He married Sarah Hillings and William jnr was born in Emerald, Queensland in July 1880. After the senior William's death in 1884 at the age of 36, Sarah married Henry West and had four more children – George, Harriett, Henry jnr and Elizabeth.

Henry West snr's first contact with Lord Howe Island was on 30 July 1870. Six days earlier the barque *Aurifera* sprang a leak, while sailing from Newcastle to New Caledonia, and sank 480 kms from the Island. Abandoning the stricken vessel her fourteen crew, including the cook Henry West, finally reached Lord Howe Island in a lifeboat. Signing on as cook on the *Mary Ogilvie,* Henry made further trips to the Island before settling with his family on a portion of Mosely Park in 1894. After Sarah's death in 1898 Henry and two of the children, George and Elizabeth, moved to Norfolk Island and eventually settled in New Zealand.

In 1899 William Retmock jnr married Mary Challis Nichols, eldest daughter of Tom and Mary. Their house, Alma, was built where the Doctor's residence is today. Gordon, the younger of their two sons, contracted peritonitis after an appendix operation and died on the mainland in 1929 at the age of 15. He was buried in the grave of his grandmother, Mary Nichols, at Sutherland cemetery in Sydney.

Harriett became the wife of Herbert Wilson, first-born son of T B and Mary, and had four children. Their only daughter died as a youngster. They later divorced but both remarried. Harriett married Jack Williams, a retired dentist. There were no children. Herbert wed Lillian, daughter of Ned and Janet King. Four children were born of that union.

Henry jnr married Hilda Thompson, a granddaughter of Nathan and Bokue. Their only child, Dulcie, is the wife of Les King, grandson of Ned and Janet and nephew of Lillian.

George Garth captained the schooners *Mary Ogilvie, Onward* and *Oscar Robinson* to the Island before settling there with his family in 1894. For several years they lived on an area just north of Mosely Park. Garths Fishing Place, an area halfway between Blinky Beach and Muttonbird Point, was named after Captain Garth. In 1897 his daughter Gwendolyne married George Nichols, fourth son of Mary and Tom. They had four children.

Alexander Fenton was born in Dundee, Scotland, in 1860 but spent most of his childhood in Sweden. His father, William, was employed in a business tasked with improving the quality of cotton belting for woollen mill machinery. Upon leaving Sweden, William eventually established the Cleckheaton Woollen Mills in Yorkshire, England. Although it was a lucrative family business, Alexander was not at all interested. At the age of 23 he became the 'black sheep' of the family, preferring to travel and find his own way in the world – a path that eleven years later would lead him to Lord Howe Island. By then a landscape architect for the Sydney-based horticultural company Searle's, Alexander was sent to the Island to procure Kentia palm seeds and plants.

Upon his return to Sydney in late 1894 he married Mary Gabel, whom he had met in Melbourne. A year later they made their home on the Island. For a short time they lived on Thompson's property at Signal Point before moving to an area on Neds Beach Road, known as The Rose Bush. Eventually they laid claim to a site near Mosley Park. The family home, built in 1906, is believed to have been the first construction of a Hudson kit home. The house, known as Kentia, is next to the airport terminal and is now the property of Alexander's granddaughters, Rosemary Sinclair and Robyn 'Widge' Curtin. Their brother, Stanley Fenton, also holds part of the land Alexander settled – on an area once occupied by Captain Garth.

Alexander and Mary had four children. Mary died in 1907. Alexander then married Ellen Mooney and had another son. Their grandson Esven lives on the Island today.

On 18 September 1895 the brigantine *Zeno* was carrying a cargo of coal from Newcastle to New Zealand, when she sprang a leak in heavy seas several miles off Lord Howe Island. The captain and crew abandoned the vessel minutes before she sank and rowed to the safety of Neds Beach. The crew returned to the mainland except for another 'wandering' Scotsman – 25 year-old Hector Innes who fell in love with Grace Nichols. Of their four children, the eldest lost his life in World War I.

Shortly after Nathan Thompson's death in 1895, Isabella Hansen was employed to help look after Bokue. His son William had befriended the Hansen family during his trips to Sydney. Isabella's mother, Kathleen, later died during childbirth and her father could not properly care for his family. William offered the young Isabella a home on the Island and she cared for Bokue until her death in 1897. Isabella, who was of Norwegian/Irish descent, remained on the Island and in 1899 at the age of 15, she married John Thompson (second son of Nathan and Bokue). They had eight children, two of whom died in infancy.

William Hansen followed his sister to the Island in 1902. He had been in a relationship that had produced a daughter. However, the child's mother was not permitted to marry William on religious grounds and the affair ended. William, affectionately known as 'Billy Winks', never married and remained on the Island until his death in 1972 at the age of 90.

The *Dewdrop*, a small vessel of 45 tons, anchored in Comets Hole on 22 July 1896. She was chartered for the Island trade to carry quantities of palm seeds, onions, sweet potatoes, bananas and oranges to Sydney. Her Captain, William Griffiths, was accompanied by his daughter, Amelia, who immediately caught the eye of Charles Nichols, third son of Tom and Mary. Charles and Amelia sailed to Sydney with the first shipment of produce and were married at St. Bartholomews church, Pyrmont. They returned to the Island where a son was born in 1897.

Tom Nichols captained *Dewdrop* on several trips. Upon his death in 1897 Captain Potts, an American, was given charge of the vessel and soon became the first husband of Martha Nichols, fourth daughter of Tom and Mary. Martha married twice more and had several love affairs. A Frenchman and a German were included in her conquests; and it was said she used to fly the national flag of the current incumbent from the flagpole at her home. 'Auntie Mart' died without issue in 1945. The site of her home is today the property of May Shick.

Mary Nichols, T B Wilson and John Robbins became part-owners of *Dewdrop*, which operated successfully for twelve years before they considered she was no longer a viable proposition. Burns Philp & Co then purchased her for use as a coastal trader. She was eventually wrecked on a reef off the Queensland coast.

William Whiting lived in China, where he managed a depot that sent coolies to work in the mines of Witwatersrand in South Africa. In 1897, while on the first of several visits, he met Susan, the second youngest daughter of Tom and Mary. She was still a child engaging in childhood pranks and on one occasion, after incurring William's wrath, she was on the receiving end of a good spanking. However, all was forgiven. Between his visits they corresponded until 1907 when Susan sailed to China to be married. They remained there for another two years before returning to the Island with their infant son. William and Susan's home, Palmhaven and its guest house annexe, was the first architect designed house on the Island. Situated at the top of Bowker Avenue, today it is the residence of Jan Garton.

Henry Payten, father of Harry and uncle of Phillip Dignam, was one of eleven children from a prosperous family. His father, Nathaniel Payten, amassed a fortune as a hotelier and landowner in the districts of Parramatta, Goulburn, Bathurst, Seven Hills and Guildford. He was also a well-known and highly respected identity in the pioneering days of Parramatta. As a building contractor there – between 1830 and 1850 he was credited with many of that town's better class structures. In 1846 he built the All Saints Church of England, dedicated to the memory of the Reverend Samuel Marsden.

Between 1818 and 1820, Nathaniel and a partner supervised the construction of the Parramatta Female Factory and Convict Barracks of which Governor Macquarie wrote in his diary:-

> After breakfast I went to the place selected for building the Factory and Barracks on the left bank of the Parramatta River, where I met the contractors, Messrs. Payten and Watkins. At 12 o'clock I laid the foundation stone of the new building – giving the workmen four gallons of spirits to drink to the success of the building

Nathaniel's own Parramatta home, Tara, was a 17-room stone mansion that took two years to build at a cost of £3300. From 1841 it stood for 122 years before being bulldozed in just seven hours to make way for an office block for Gestetner Ltd.

Henry, fifth son of Nathaniel, followed in his father's footsteps. After completing his education at King's College he became an affluent hotelier in Goulburn, where he married Amelia Dignam and had seven children. Balancing family and business, he deemed hotels unsuitable places to raise children and so bought a huge family estate. Many years later, Kenmore House was purchased by the Government to house the Goulburn College of Advanced Education. Henry also owned The Towers, a large property outside Goulburn that later became a convent.

By the 1890s Henry was a very wealthy man and could have retired. However, he invested his fortune in a fellmongering business and lost practically everything in just a few years. From 1896 to 1899 he held the licence of the Commercial Hotel at Milton. By then a widower he retired to Lord Howe Island, which he had visited on a whaling expedition with his son and nephew many years before. Soon after his arrival he married Mabel, eldest daughter of T B and Mary Wilson, and fifty years his junior. They had three sons. A few years after Henry's death in 1906 Mabel married her stepson, Harry. Of their two children a daughter died in infancy.

Phillip Payten and Susan Andrews, two of Henry's children from his marriage to Amelia Dignam, also settled on the Island. Phillip, a retired surveyor who had several streets in the Sydney Metropolitan area named after him, co-founded the Bowling Club with his brother Harry. Susan, a widow known as 'Auntie May' died in 1932 at the age of 45.

As the Payten sons grew to adulthood and had families of their own, they built their homes on a large area that became known as Paytens Selection. The sites are mostly

Four generations of the Wilson family, circa 1927
T B and Mary (seated), daughter Mabel, grandson Frank,
great-grandaughters, Jean (on T B's knee) and Beryl

John and Isabella Thompson and family, circa 1925
Maude, Elsie, Gladys, Hilda, Daisy and John jnr

tourist resorts today. Donald, a grandson of Henry, owns Beachcomber; John Green, a great-grandson, owns Earls Anchorage; and Broken Banyan is the site of the property once owned by Henry's son, Tom.

In 1900, George Massy Kirby visited the Island on the persuasion of his friend and former shipmate, William Whiting. Upon his arrival, Mary Nichols decided the Irishman was the most eligible male around and informed him he would marry her favourite daughter, Edith. Mary was not a woman to be trifled with and George dutifully complied, marrying Edith in January 1902. They had two sons. George was a very formal and proper man who usually dressed in a white suit and straw hat and always smoked a pipe. As a teacher for 20 years, he had a profound influence on the Island children.

Edward Austic also arrived in 1900 and six years later became the second husband of Rosario Hamill (nee Thompson). They had three daughters one of whom died in infancy. In 1909 Edward's sister Ada married Gower Wilson, second son of T B and Mary. Their marriage produced seven children. Tragically, Gower and his eldest son Jack, were lost at sea in 1936 in the same disaster that claimed the life of William Hamill.

The last of the settlers who defined the Island's geneaology for several generations was Robert Baxter, a 20 year-old employee of the Sydney Telephone Company. He planned only a short visit but fell in love with the Island and, more importantly, one of its lovely ladies. Robert took Ethel Robbins, daughter of John and Mary, back to the mainland where they married. Soon after, they returned to the Island to settle and raise five children. The original Baxter home, Redlands, is today the home of Norma Whitfield.

As the eldest daughter of Robert and Ethel, and like the children born before her who were given names in honour of ships and captains – Ysobel was named after the ship that brought her father to her mother.

TRAGEDY OF THE 'SYLPH'

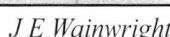

J E Wainwright

Captain William Field

The hopes and dreams of a better life on Lord Howe Island were shattered forever for three families with the tragic loss of the *Sylph*.

William Field, an American Captain on the barque *Woodlark* and a former acquaintance of Nathan Thompson, made the Island his home in January 1855. His wife, Mary, followed two years later. They built a house on Nathan's property opposite Signal Point where evidence of Captain Field's well still exists. A devoted couple, they worked hard and were highly respected in the community.

Thomas Mooney arrived with his wife Mary on the schooner *Bluebell* in 1867. They established a farm on a portion of the Andrews' property towards Nichols Clear Place and soon began raising a family.

Henry Wainwright, a carpenter from London, settled with his wife, Jane Elizabeth (known as J E) and two children, in 1868. They claimed a portion of land on a point overlooking a secluded spot known today as Lovers Bay. He farmed and raised livestock, introducing cows to the Island in 1870.

When Water Police Magistrate P J Cloete undertook a police investigation in 1869, he wrote of the Islanders: -

> About 33 acres of land are under cultivation and producing good crops of potatoes, maize, onions, cabbages, oranges, lemons, bananas, peaches, grapes, arrowroot and coffee – all thrive exceedingly well but the inhabitants care little to cultivate more than just sufficient for their wants. The only produce they export is onions, which are brought to Sydney in a small ketch (the Sylph), the joint property of Thompson, Wainwright and Field. There is excellent fishing and turkeys, ducks, fowls, etc. are reared in great numbers.

The *Sylph* was built in Brisbane in 1845 and sailed as far as the Galapagos Islands, before operating as a NSW coastal trader in the 1850s. Concerned over the declining whaling trade, Nathan Thompson purchased the *Sylph* in 1867. As the first locally owned vessel to trade between Lord Howe and Sydney, she made many trips carrying passengers and produce, chiefly onions and pigs. Although only a small vessel, *Sylph* proved too big for Nathan to handle alone. After an incident when she broke her moorings and stranded on the reef he enlisted the aid of Captain Field and Henry Wainwright to free her, offering them a share in the business for their trouble.

Sylph ran successfully until her final voyage on 20 April 1873. Lost at sea, she took with her Captain Field, Thomas Mooney and Henry Wainwright's family. After learning of her disappearance, searches carried out by other vessels failed to find her. However, a report handed in by Captain Lake of the SS *Boomerang* on 17 June 1873 stated: -

> passed a small vessel bottom up with the mainmast broken off short by the deck; masthead cap., and crosstree gone; lower part of the mast painted white; sail apparently blown away; vessel coppered; top sides black, rudder unshipped. Owing to it being late in the day and a squall coming on, with high seas running, unable to lower a boat to ascertain name. The above mentioned spars were alongside and fast to the vessel. The keel of the vessel was about 50 ft. long, with round forefoot and square stern beam about 12 ft.

This wreckage was sighted off Double Island, part of the Beverley Group, which is about 100 kms off the Queensland coast. Whether it was the *Sylph* or not was never established. Experienced mariners at the time said that *Sylph's* mainsail was far too big for her and her loss may have been caused from being over-sparred.

Captain Field and Mary had no children. Mary, who was born in Dublin, did not remarry. Impoverished in her final years, and living off the charity of other Islanders, she died on 24 November 1896 aged 79 years. Today, the site William and Mary lived on is the property of Michael Thompson.

The Mooney's three children were Patrick, Thomas and Ellen. Patrick, born in 1868, was a popular lad who, after accompanying Ned King on an ascent of Mount Lidgbird, became affectionately known as Paddy the First. Perhaps through the loss of his father he became prone to anti-social behaviour, and at the age of 26 was committed to the mental institute at Morriset where he died a few years later. Thomas died in 1871 at the age of 9 months. Ellen, born in 1872, shortly before the loss of her father, became the second wife of Alexander Fenton.

Mary Mooney remarried but while her first marriage certificate, still in possession of her great-grandson, Esven, bears her signature, only an 'X' marks the certificate of her second marriage in 1880 to John Robbins. Some claimed she signed the latter that way out of loyalty to Thomas, in the belief he would one day return to her.

Henry, stricken with grief, waited in vain for his family to return. However, he did not long survive the loss of his wife and children. He died from an accident just a few years later. Some older Islanders claimed his burial site somewhere in the vicinity of Lovers Bay gave rise to its name, while others were certain his remains lay in an unmarked grave in the Thompson cemetery.

Sylph's anchorage was in a deep part of the water off Old Settlement Beach. Named Sylphs Hole, it is still a reminder of those who lost their lives on her.

OTHER SETTLERS

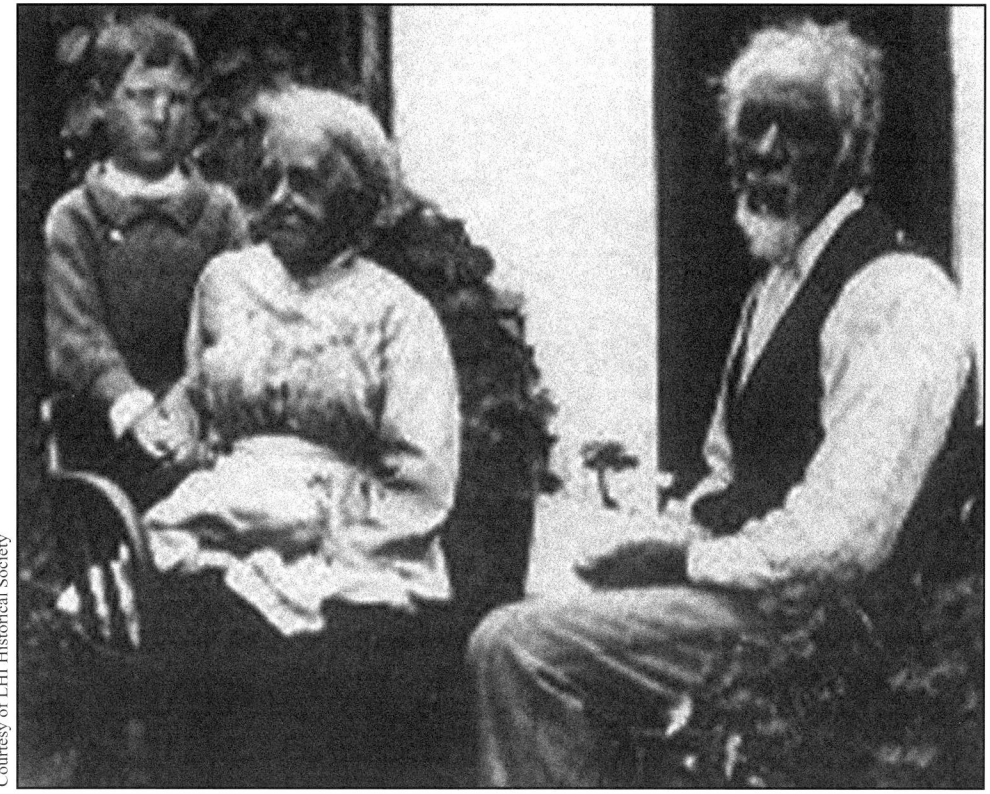

Courtesy of LHI Historical Society

Frank 'Cobby' Robbins with Sarah and Perry Johnson

T he Lord Howe Island lifestyle was not what many early settlers expected, and some stayed only a short time. Others remained a lifetime but having no children their names are no longer linked with Island families today.

In September 1855 the schooner *Will O' the Wisp* called in for provisions while returning to New Zealand from a fishing expedition at Elizabeth Reef. Soon after, the vessel's master, Captain Stevens, returned with his 10 year-old son, Campbell, and acquired Captain Middleton's property at North Bay. Accompanying them were a Maori servant, Jacky Wahoo, and an American negro, Perry Johnson.

Campbell later attended school in New Zealand, after which he enlisted in the Militia during the second of the Maori Wars. Returning to the Island in 1870, he married Alice Leonard the following year. They remained on the Stevens farm at North Bay until

1882 when a Government appointed position took them to the main settlement area. Campbell died in Sydney in 1930. Stevens Reserve and Stevens Point, the first point south of Hells Gates (between Neds Beach and Middle Beach), were named after him.

Perry Johnson escaped his life of slavery in America by running away to sea. As a crewman on whaling ships, he eventually reached New Zealand where he signed on as mate on *Will O' the Wisp*. Some time after settling on the Island with Captain Stevens, he visited Sydney and brought back a Cape Negress named Sarah.

Sarah Rachel Mitchell, a Hottentot, was born in the Cape of Good Hope Colony in South Africa. Orphaned at the age of 5, she was adopted and raised in Hong Kong. Well educated and employed as a governess/house nurse, she transferred to Sydney where she met and fell in love with Perry. Captain Field officiated at their marriage in 1860. Fifty-three years later, on being told their union was not legal, they were officially married by Pastor Edwin Butz.

Like the Moselys, Perry and Sarah probably felt compelled to legalise their union on religious grounds. It was not until 1878 that the first resident Registrar for Births, Deaths & Marriages was appointed. Before that time, marriages conducted on the Island by whaling captains were of doubtful legality. Ship captains were empowered to conduct such ceremonies but only while on the high seas. However, in the early days of settlement, with no clergyman or other officials on the Island, couples either went to the mainland to find a church; or accepted the pronouncements of whaling captains.

After leaving Captain Stevens' employ, Perry worked as Nathan's farm labourer, while Sarah tended the cattle and helped as a domestic in the Thompson home. Eventually they established their own farm at the foot of Mount Lidgbird, where the landmarks of Johnsons Beach, Johnsons Reef and Johnsons Point take their name. Their farm included a large peach orchard. Consequently, the ridge extending from Big Creek to the summit of Intermediate Hill was known for many years as Peach Tree Ridge. Perry died in December 1915 aged 83. Sarah, affectionately known as 'Auntie Johnson', died in April 1918 aged 100.

William Gibson spent nine years on the Island before selling his holdings to Captain Starich of the vessel *Gleaner* in 1865. Starich employed an English couple, John and Ellen Lewis, to manage the property until he retired from his life at sea in 1871. However, he also left after a few years, transferring his holdings to Margaret Andrews who willed it to her daughter, Mary. It was later apportioned to Grace Nichols upon her marriage to Hector Innes. Their daughter, Jean, eventually inherited the property which was demolished in 1973 to make way for the Island's airstrip.

David Whybrow, Captain of the brig *Curlew*, arrived with his wife, three children and a grandchild in 1858. They farmed a site that became known as Whybrow Ridge. This ridge extends from the northern slope of Intermediate Hill, known as North Hummock, to Johnsons Point. The Captain continued whaling during their nineteen year tenure on the Island, leaving the responsibility of the family and farm to Tom, his 18 year-old son. Tom loved the hills, the mountains, and hunting. He became an experienced bushman, assisting Ned King as a mountain guide for visiting survey expeditions. Whybrow Ridge, no longer known by that name, is today the site of several private homes and the tourist resort Capella.

After making several visits to the Island in the 1850s, Captain William Osborn Spurling was offered a portion of Nathan Thompson's land in 1861. Captain Spurling became the first postmaster and held the honorary position until his return to the mainland in 1879.

Charles Williams, a whaler on the English barque *Tigress*, made the first of many trips in 1840 before establishing a farm on the Island in 1866. Mary Nichols, whose holdings north of The Pines bordered Williams' farm, wanted to buy his property for several years. She was reported to have said: -

If I can't buy him out I'll blow him out

In trying to 'blow' Charles out, under Mary's instructions her workers continually demolished his windbreaks between the two properties. Her attempts to acquire the farm were in vain. However, her efforts may have proven too much for an old mariner. In 1891 he sold his farm to a young man who was not one to be reckoned with. Mary would never blow Philip Dignam out.

Charles Williams stayed on as a tenant on the Dignam property. And, Mary must have forgiven him for his obstinacy, for upon his death in 1892 he was laid to rest in the Pinetrees cemetery.

Bill Brown, a whaler from the Isle of Wight, worked for Margaret Andrews during his eleven years residency. He died on the Island in April 1882 and is believed to be buried in one of the unmarked graves in Pinetrees cemetery.

The Searle family, which included ten children, arrived about 1870 bringing with them their horse and a ton of flour. With no house to live in, they relied on the generosity of the Johnsons, who often gave temporary lodgings to new settlers. However, disillusioned and daunted by the prospect of having to build a home, the family soon tired of the Island life. Unfortunately, on the voyage back to Sydney there was no accommodation on the ship and they had to endure the trip in the hold.

Geordie King and his family were also guests of Perry and Sarah, until they built a house nearby. Alas, shortly after moving into their new home, it was destroyed by a waterspout and they returned to the mainland.

Joseph Lucas began farming a portion of land adjoining Captain Starich's property in 1871. However, after six years he sold his holdings to Margaret Andrews and returned to sea. The property later became the home of Margaret's great-grandson, Alec Innes, son of Grace and Hector. When the house was demolished for construction of the airstrip Alec's widow, Vera (daughter of Phillip and Emeline Dignam), relocated to the property of their daughter, Mavis Fitzgerald, owner of Waimarie Holiday Apartments.

A man known only as Jenkins was a whaler on the *Jane,* before enlisting as mate on the *Comet.* When that vessel ceased operation in 1876 Jenkins settled on the Island, establishing a farm near Charles Williams' property. However, he too tired of the Island lifestyle and in 1878 sold his farm to Margaret Andrews. That same year, Margaret transferred all her holdings to her daughter Mary. The former Jenkins property was later apportioned to her son, George, upon his marriage to Gwendolyne in 1897. After George's death in 1947 his house, known as Maelgwyn, was purchased by the Board of Control for a teacher's residence. The area George and his family once occupied today encompasses Blue Peters and the surrounding area.

Englishman Henry Wilson (no relation to T B) commenced residency in 1872, eventually building a small house on Mosely's land. Henry had been a member of one of the forty Arctic expeditions sent in search of the British explorer, Sir John Franklin. In 1845, Franklin and 129 men set out on the ships *Erebus* and *Terror* in a quest to find the Northwest Passage. In what became one of the greatest Arctic tragedies, Franklin and his party perished after their ships were frozen in ice.

Henry, a keen sportsman, introduced the game of cricket to the Island. However, in the early 1890s he was suspected of having leprosy and forced to leave. Fearing an epidemic, the Islanders burnt his house and belongings. Fortunately, it was not leprosy but he did not return to the Island, possibly because he had nothing left to return to.

The Lord family arrived in 1880 and established a farm on Whybrow Ridge, known as Lords Garden. A group of rocks off Johnsons Point were also given their name. However, they stayed only eight months. Upon their departure, John and Mary Robbins purchased the property and extended their farming activities to both sides of the ridge as well as the area once occupied by Henry Wainwright. The latter site became known as Robbins Point. Their family home passed down to Mary's daughter, Ellen, and then to her son, Norman Fenton. The original 'house of Lords' is today the home of Pixie and Eddie Rourke. Norman's son, Esven, also owns a portion of the original property, with much of the land once farmed by John Robbins forming part of his Special lease.

John and Charles Mason, employees of Henderson & MacFarland, were sent to the Island in 1881 when the Government granted a licence for that Company to collect guano for shipment to New Zealand. The business failed but John and Charles eventually made the Island their home. Over sixty years later 'Mr Bush', the son of Captain Bushell (master of the vessel used in the guano operation), also became a resident for a time, returning to his native New Zealand in 1951.

W E Langley was sent to the Island in 1882 as a correspondent for the New York Herald, and again in 1884 as editor of the Illustrated Sydney News. Langley was appointed Registrar of Births, Deaths & Marriages in 1885, a position he held until his death in 1894. He was buried in the Thompson cemetery.

Captain Charles Darthe, James Tyrell and Alan Harland sailed to the Island on the ketch *Bound to Win* in November 1889 for a shipment of palm seeds. A few months later they returned on Harland's own ketch *Welcome Home*, bringing his wife and nine children with them. Harland had entered into a farming partnership with Charles Williams. Captain Darthe agreed to operate the vessel as a carrier for their produce while James Tyrell was employed as a farm hand. However, the venture was short-lived. In February 1891 Darthe set sail for Norfolk Island and was never seen again. Harland, financially ruined by the loss of his vessel, took his family back to the mainland.

James Tyrell then worked for Nathan Thompson before signing on as mate on the schooner *Friendship*. Later Mary Nichols, on learning that he had married and wished to return to the Island, offered him employment. James and his wife eventually built a home in an area near the public cemetery known as The Lemon Trees. A talented musician, Hester Tyrell was popular in the Island's social scene and gave music lessons to many young Islanders. They left the Island in 1915.

From 1895 to 1910, George Waterhouse occupied a large tract of land behind The Pines. As owner of the vessel *Dewdrop,* he offered a partnership to three residents and led a very comfortable existence as a farmer, while numerous captains operated the vessel between the Island and Sydney. George was also a shareholder in the fledgling palm seed export industry.

At the time of *Dewdrop's* departure in 1908, steamship trade had been established between Sydney, Lord Howe Island and Norfolk Island. And another five decades would pass before the Islanders again relied on small commercial vessels for trade with the mainland.

10

ROGUES IN PARADISE

Captains on whalers were not noted for enforcing, nor their men for abiding by the more conventional rules observed by officers and their crews on warships. While most of Lord Howe Island's salty pioneers were responsible and well-behaved, with the added invaluable knack at odd jobs, there were a few exceptions. Some whalers grew tired of their arduous seafaring existence and, lured by the Island's easy-going charm, readily deserted their ships. However, the Utopian lifestyle they expected was just an illusion.

PRISON IN A BARREL

In 1844, Moss, the first of these deserters, refused to work for his keep. Captain Poole convened a 'court' in which the little community judged Moss to be an undesirable character. Poole subsequently ordered his deportation. On learning of his fate, Moss became aggressive and threatened to burn down the houses and store. As it was not known when the next ship would call; and with a lack of incarceration facilities, his jurists decided to chain him to a palm tree. One night he managed to break free of his tethers and escaped to the bush. Believing he would make good his threats, the buildings were surrounded with casks of water and a 24-hour watch was kept.

However, apart from bombarding the settlement with rocks, Moss inflicted little damage and was finally captured.

He was then confined in crudely made stocks but after several days it was decided that this type of punishment might cripple him, so another mode of captivity was adopted. Moss was placed into a large oil barrel fitted with a makeshift trapdoor; to allow eating and drinking vessels to be passed to him. Whether he was allowed out for a pee, or whatever, is not known but the cask was his prison for several weeks.

Still in his barrel, Moss was finally shipped to Sydney but it was Poole who was subsequently charged with an offence. However, he bought Moss off for £10 and the case was dismissed. Blackmail could have followed as it would eventually cost Poole another £40 before he was finally rid of him!

THE LEGEND OF BLACK BILLY

An incident in the middle 1850s involving two deserters became part of Island folklore. 'Black Billy', a descendant from Tasmanian aboriginals, deserted the *Aladdin* and was given employment by the Andrews family. One day he and another employee, named Williams, went pig and goat hunting. That evening Williams returned alone saying he had last seen his companion at the Smoking Tree. Black Billy was never seen again but eleven days later his dog returned, very thin and sporting injuries consistent with having been tied up. Suspicions were aroused. The community accused Williams of foul play, informing him that the matter would be referred to the captain of the next warship to visit the Island. Williams did not wait around. Seeking berth on the next provisioning whaler, he claimed he was heading for South America to open a barber's shop in Valparaiso! Williams was not heard of again and Black Billy's fate remains a mystery.

The Smoking Tree Ridge extends from the north side of Mount Lidgbird to Intermediate Hill. Pig hunters and seed collectors regularly stopped for 'smoko' at a large sallywood, known as the smoking tree, on the crest of the ridge. Returning home from a long day in the hills, it was their custom to fire a gun from the tree as a signal for 'Auntie Johnson' to put the kettle on for a cup of tea. Over the years, many who rested at the smoking tree claimed to have seen the ghost of Black Billy.

THE GHOST TREE

The next chapter of Lord Howe Island's folklore began in 1862 on a portion of land north of Charles Williams' property. It was there that David Lloyd settled with his wife Mary, and daughter Alice. Two years later Alice married John Leonard, an American from Lowell in Massachusetts, who had deserted from the whaler *Gayhead*. In 1869 Leonard had a violent quarrel with his father-in-law and attacked him. In the ensuing fight Lloyd defended himself with a knife, fatally wounding Leonard. The incident prompted a newspaper of the day to report: -

And where the great countries had their wars, this island had its one murder

Water Police Magistrate P J Cloete was sent to the Island on the Government steamer *Thetis* to investigate the death, and subsequently ruled the incident justifiable homicide. In his report on the matter, the Magistrate wrote: -

Lloyd killed his son-in-law, a wastrel of a fellow from an American whaler. If the old man had chosen to hide in those dark mountains – Lidgbird or Gower no man could have found him. But he had given himself up and seemed to have been first assaulted before he stabbed the other.

When David and Mary left in 1871 Alice had married Campbell Stevens, and she remained on the Island until her death in the early 1920s.

For many years Islanders claimed to have seen Leonard's ghost, or felt his presence, near an old greybark tree that stood on the spot where he was killed. The tree is no longer there, but some older residents still recall being told by their parents to avoid the ghost tree.

PROWLERS

Alec 'Scottie' Frazer and William Chapman deserted from the whaler *Especulador* in 1881. It is unknown where they lived but, preferring not to work, they slept during the day and prowled around people's homes at night. Although not confined to prison barrels, they too were deported after Chapman tried to claim Lords Garden, then owned by John and Mary Robbins.

BLACKBIRDERS

Not all the rogues were deserters. When the Government appointed Captain Armstrong as the first Administrator on the Island in 1878, his recruitment of cheap labour did not sit well with the Islanders. As the Captain's business interests expanded he employed kanakas from Noumea. One of the natives, Charley Noddy, claimed that pearls were to be found in the Island's clams and, with his employer's permission, he opened hundreds of them. Evidence of this destruction could still be seen near the south reef for many years. Although Armstrong claimed to have hired the kanakas legally under licence from the French authorities; some believed he bought them through Pacific pirates known as *blackbirders*.

In September 1881 four more young men, originally from the Malabar Coast of India, were also brought in from New Caledonia. They too were thought to have been bought from the slavers; to serve as labourers in the collection of guano. Some time later, while trying to gather some of the beautiful tail feathers from the bosun birds nesting at the summit of North Peak, one of the Indians, Hielavapa, missed his footing and plummeted to his death. His body was recovered and he was buried in Pinetrees cemetery. The peak was renamed Malabar after that accident.

Blackbirding began in the early 1860s, at a time when the American Civil War was being fought to free slaves. Pirates bought, kidnapped or bribed Melanesian natives into a life of virtual slavery on the Australian mainland and Fiji. From the time it began until finally prohibited in 1889, the trade uprooted 100,000 natives from their islands. Of that number, 60,000 were forced into the Queensland cane fields.

Although the traffic of natives was an accepted practice, it produced many low cutthroats. Legal action against ships' captains for the brutal treatment of natives was commonplace in Sydney courts. One such case, against the 48-ton schooner *Daphne* seized for piracy by HMS *Rosario* in 1871, was dismissed. Captain Palmer of the latter ship was ordered to pay the court costs, while the *Daphne* continued to ply her trade. However, the public outcry which followed the case eventually forced the State Governments to strengthen their laws on native recruitment.

HMS Rosario overhauling the slaver Carl

THE VERNON BOYS

In 1881 Captain Armstrong apprenticed five boys from *Vernon*, Australia's first Nautical School Ship. A former East Indian paddle steamer she was purchased by the NSW Government, converted to full sail and refitted as a training ship for homeless, neglected and destitute boys as young as two years. Once they turned seventeen, the boys were apprenticed to other ships. The Islanders objected strongly to the presence of 'juvenile delinquents' but to no avail. The Commander of their host ship, HMS *Alacrity,* informed them that the boys would be landed by force if necessary. Landed they were and there they stayed until 1882.

In September 1881 Armstrong recommended to the Council of Education that Robert Rose, another of his employees, should be appointed T B Wilson's successor as schoolmaster. Although the Department endorsed the recommendation, Rose declined the position because of his association with the Vernon boys who had been placed under his charge for the previous 5 months. He knew that if he accepted the position, the Islanders would withdraw their support for the school.

THE BIGAMIST

In December 1881 Armstrong nominated William Clarson, an acquaintance from the mainland, for the position of teacher stating that he had known him for some years and that he was: -

> well capable of undertaking such duties as are required – he has many advantages, he being an artist by trade and his wife I believe to be a most efficient teacher

Clarson accepted the appointment on 1 January 1882, arriving at the Island in February. However, his appointment was short-lived. On 15 May Clarson was committed for trial on a charge of bigamy, having married only eight days after he had wed another.

11

THE LEAN YEARS

Unloading the Thetis (1882)

With the decline of whaling in the 1860s, followed by the loss of the *Sylph,* the future of Lord Howe Island's farmers seemed bleak as a period of obscurity settled over them. From 1873 they depended heavily on the 92-ton *Comet* for shipping their produce to Sydney markets. By then the staple export was the Lord Howe Island Red Onion, sought after by whalers and mainland markets since the early 1850s. However by 1876 smut had decimated this once lucrative industry, and the *Comet* was forced out of business.

During the visit of HMS *Pearl* in 1876, the ship's surgeon, Alfred T Corrie, noted that some of the inhabitants were almost in a state of starvation, and in his report wrote:-

> Sometimes six or twelve months pass without a vessel calling at the Island…but now this once much frequented and favoured little spot is apparently, quite deserted; the old families have lost all zeal for cultivation, having to live as it were from hand to mouth, seeing the fruits of their labour decaying and rotting in the storehouses

Long periods between visiting ships meant selling or trading produce for commodities such as tea, sugar, salt, flour, soap and clothing was severely limited. But as for the *near state of starvation* all evidence appeared to the contrary. The Islanders endured the lean years with determination. They learned to make do with what they had; and found alternatives for what they did not have.

Alec Innes catching Muttonbirds

When flour supplies ran low they ground corn to make bread. They ate pill-eye, which was made by mixing a bucketful of grated sweet potato with a saucer of flour, a little fat, and then baked in loaves. Salt was scraped from rocks where seawater had evaporated; and sugar-cane was crushed for use as a sweetener. As a substitute for potatoes, green bananas were boiled in their skins. Sow thistle and purslane were eaten in place of cabbages. Forkedy pies made from the seeds of the pandanus (also known as the fork tree, tent tree or screw pine) became part of the Island fare for many years.

There were plenty of goats, pigs, poultry and dairy cattle. The sea offered up an endless supply of fish and other delicacies. Bêche-de-mers were a prized source of food, either boiled or eaten raw; and sea lettuce was another vegetable substitute.

The annual collection of muttonbird eggs began on 28 November and was known as Egg Day. Nests were cleared every other day throughout the following week, ensuring the freshness of the eggs. Armed with buckets, Islanders gathered them from nest-holes around Neds Beach and on Malabar. At the end of each collection, a tally was taken after which a number of eggs were apportioned to each family. The remainder were stacked in barrels between layers of coarse salt, which preserved them for up to six weeks.

Young muttonbirds were also common fare. Soaked in brine, then hung on racks in smokehouses or on gosshooks in the chimneys above open fires, the birds were dehydrated by the heat and cured by various tars and resins in the smoke. This process preserved the flesh from one season to the next. The carcasses also provided another use – the dark coloured oil extracted from them was used for lighting.

A shrubby melaleuca, known as kilmogue, tasted like tea; and geranium leaves were a substitute for tobacco. A potent Island mixture brewed from bananas and wild figs supplemented the limited supplies of alcohol.

While Islanders still possessed their Sunday best from a more profitable era, working clothes were needed. Goatskins were treated and fashioned into moccasins. Flour bags were used to make shirts, trousers, smocks and caps.

As a result of Alfred Corrie's report in 1876, the Government considered removing the Island's inhabitants to the mainland. This prompted a second visit by Surveyor Fitzgerald, who arrived with Captain Amora on the schooner *Esperanza* on 26 November 1876. In a letter to the Sydney Morning Herald, dated 12 January 1877, Fitzgerald wrote of his visit: -

As an example of the supposed distress of the Lord Howe Islanders, the bill of fare must be given. Bluefish, Garfish, Salmon, Rockcod, Parrot fish etc. – sucking-pig and pig that might have been sucked for anything known to the contrary; kid, and possibly goat (that the legation could not tell from mutton); poultry in all forms including eggs in all shapes; peach pies and puddings of all sorts, sweet potatoes, 'Irish' potatoes, maize, fried bananas, palm cabbage, butter, milk, with other things eaten then but now forgotten.

As to the object of the mission – it being to enquire into the supposed state of the inhabitants, to promise their removal, if necessary, and to establish, if possible, communication and trade with Sydney – much need not be said here. Further than, that the wants of those residing on the island (forty in number) were ready money – owing to the failure of the onion crops – new clothes, owing to the first want, and whalers not having called – tea, sugar, flour and tobacco, owing to such articles not being produced on the island.

No one desired to be resumed, and the preliminary steps are now being taken to re-establish a whaling and fishing station on the island, to promote a trade by the planting of coffee (which grows luxuriantly) by the introduction of similar products, and the regular shipment to Sydney of such things that are now available, including fungus for the Celestials (Chinese).

The politics are simple (without a responsible Government) and consequently satisfactory.

Anyone may call a meeting and the minority (without speaking against time) gives way to the majority.

To arrange terms with Captain Amora several such meetings were held, at which I was present, some of them extending into the small hours of the morning, and in my opinion were characterized by great decorum, moderation and good temper, while some of the speaking was decidedly effective.

If I were not in the employment of the Government, I might be tempted here to draw a contrast – but never mind.

Since a former visit a great boon has been conferred upon the residents by the introduction (by Mr. Wainwright) of cattle, and it is really wonderful to see the milch cows (cows giving two buckets of milk a day) tethered to a stake and as fat as prize oxen. There being no timber that will last for any time in the ground, a fence necessitates the use of a chain. Another great improvement has been made under a law precluding the keeping of tame goats or pigs, unless in a sty. The wild goats are much reduced in number.

In a further letter, dated 13 February 1877, Fitgerald wrote: -

> Coffee plants grow well, though evidently neglected, and I have little doubt that coffee might be made an important item in the trade of the island.
>
> I therefore promised (subject to approval) that 100 plants would be sent from the Botanical Gardens as an experiment, together with some shelter plants, which are much required.
>
> Should it be determined that such plants be forwarded they should, it is recommended, be consigned equally to Mr. E. King and Captain Thompson, elected by the inhabitants to take charge of them, and to these donations some few other tropical plants and seeds might be added with advantage.

Approval was given and, on 16 April 1877, the Botanical Gardens despatched the coffee plants plus as assortment of other plants including: -

> Kei apple, fig, yellow guava, passionfruit, jack fruit, wine palm, thyme, lavender, marjoram, sage, mint, turmeric, cinnamon, sarsparilla, chickory, liquorice, tea, black walnut, loquat, brazillian cherry, black guava, hops, arrowroot, horehound, winter savoury and sea kale.

In return, between 1880 and 1898, Ned King supplied the Botanical Gardens with a variety of the Island's plant and bird life. In one five-year period he sent: -

> 1005 plants – including palms, pandanus and ferns
> 47 dried specimens of plants
> 17 bushels of palm seed – forsteriana, canterburyana, belmoreana
> 6 bags of soil
> 4 woodhens

Fitzgerald was sure an important trade in coffee could be established, but it was not to be. By then the diversity and richness of the Island's native flora and fauna were attracting outside attention. Of particular interest was a beautiful palm – a palm that would one day grace luxury hotels, ballrooms and salons around the world. The era of the Kentia palm seed trade was dawning.

Following Surveyor Fitzgerald's report, the removal of the Islanders was deemed unnecessary. Instead, in 1878, the Government proclaimed Lord Howe Island a Forest Reserve; and instated its own representative to take full control of Island affairs. However, this appointment would not last and, although periods of hardship continued, the Islanders managed to get by. G. Rankin, during his visit on *Thetis* in

1882, wrote:-

There is something wonderfully suggestive in the fact that 13 households support themselves from 800 acres of soil, without the aid of any land law at all. The seasons come and go; the corn and bananas ripen, the cows give milk; the rain falls, and the grass grows, without any printed forms, and entirely independent of all Occupation and Alienation acts.

In a deposition to a 1911 Royal Commission into the control of the Kentia Palm seed trade, visiting Magistrate Frank Farnell said that, on his first visit to the Island in 1900, he found the inhabitants were: -

poverty stricken…and bearing evidences of the neglect of the Government to take any interest in the Islanders

By 1900 a steamer link from Sydney had been established, bringing Lord Howe Island's first tourists. Poverty would have almost certainly been a deterrent to those early visitors, who warmed to the hospitality of the residents; and the settlers who continued to arrive until 1905. However, through mismanagement, the Islanders' venture into the export of palm seed was not yielding the just rewards; and money was still scarce. Consequently, they still relied heavily on farming for most of their needs – on land to which they had no title.

Loading seeds for shipment to Sydney

THE ARMSTRONG INQUIRY

Captain Richard Armstrong   *John Bowie Wilson*

Following the proclamation of Lord Howe Island as a Forest Reserve in 1878 Captain Richard Armstrong, a retired naval officer, was appointed Forest Ranger, Registrar of Births, Deaths & Marriages, followed by Postmaster in early 1879. Later that year he was also instated as Resident Magistrate, Coroner and Clerk of Petty Sessions, taking his annual income to over £300, plus his navy pension.

To add to his princely income, Armstrong was granted leasehold of 100 acres at an annual rental of 5 shillings. The lease was to be used for cultivation purposes; and for working the fibre from the leaf base of the Kentia palm for export to the mainland. It is believed his leasehold extended from what is today the northern boundary of Thornleigh to the Powerhouse, and through land surrounded by Anderson Road. Those areas now encompass Blue Lagoon Lodge, Somerset Apartments, Howeana, Banyan Garden, the Board Nursery and Research Centre, Earls Anchorage and its adjoining properties.

Captain Richard Ramsay Armstrong had a distinguished naval career, beginning in 1847 as a cadet on HMS *Howe*. The following year, as a midshipman on the same vessel, he was appointed aide-de-camp to Queen Adelaide (consort to King William 1V) during her tour of Lisbon and Madeira. He served on the West African coast in the suppression of slavery and in the Crimean War. During that conflict he was promoted to Lieutenant Commander; and decorated for gallantry by France (Knight of the Legion of Honour) and Turkey (Order of the Médjidié). He was wounded three times and as a result of his injuries was discharged from active service, returning to England in 1856.

In 1864 he was posted to the Canterbury province of New Zealand as Chief Immigration Officer, Commissioner & Inspector of Immigrant Ships and Administrator of Charitable Aid. After leaving New Zealand in 1867 he invested in a copra plantation in Fiji. He eventually settled with his family in New South Wales, where he unsuccessfully invested in the development of several mines.

Captain Armstrong was requested by the NSW Government to visit Lord Howe Island in 1878, to investigate an alleged disturbance between the Island's inhabitants and the captain and crew of the schooner *Mary Peverly*. His handling of this investigation led to his official appointment later that year. His wife remained in Sydney with their two sons, both of whom were at university.

Armstrong introduced many initiatives to benefit the Islanders in the wake of the depression that had descended upon them with the decline of the whaling trade. He secured Government approval and assistance for the opening of a school. He planted a variety of trees. He implemented more efficient farming methods and experimented with many new crops. He encouraged the Islanders to export palm seed, palm fibre and pandanus seed. He built the first road, Shore Road, known now as Lagoon Road. In 1880 he dynamited rocks obstructing the northern entrance to the Lagoon, creating the principal entrance, the North Passage. He obtained Government boats and moorings for the Islanders; and by 1882 his plans for the construction of a jetty were under consideration. Armstrong also had charge of the Island's liquor supply.

Soon after his arrival, the small steamer *Eva* was driven onto the reef as she was seeking passage into the Lagoon. The sea was too rough for the Islanders to get a boat close to her, but they ventured as far as they could. Then Captain Armstrong, in fine naval tradition, stripped to the waist and with a line securing him to the boat, ploughed into the heavy surf. Upon reaching the stricken vessel, he was dragged on board nearly exhausted. However, his efforts enabled the *Eva* and her crew to be towed to safety.

The Sydney Botanical Gardens, as it had done with Ned King and Nathan Thompson, supplied Captain Armstrong with a quantity of plants that included: -

Oak tree, blue gum, camphor laurel, oleander, agave, smilax, tea, coffee, Indian tea, asparagus, Brazilian cherry, fig, lemon balm, mint, thyme, oregano, salvie, lavender, cardarmon and cinnamon

The Brisbane Botanical Gardens also supplied him with a variety of plants. In return, he supplied both Gardens with samples of the Island's flora and fauna.

While some Islanders supported Armstrong and his programs, others were suspicious and resentful of his presence. Whether it was the granting of such large leasehold, the perceived threat to their own enterprises, or Government interference in their affairs; this ill-feeling would bring about Armstrong's downfall through a very public and messy inquiry.

His Government grant of 100 acres was a bitter pill for the Islanders to swallow. When they subsequently requested security of tenure over the land they had lived on, loved and cultivated for more than quarter of a century, the Government responded by commissioning a survey of their land, under 'clause 38 of the Crown Lands Occupation Act, 1875 for cultivation purposes'.

The survey, carried out by Thomas Berry in November 1880, also included areas designated by Armstrong for a public cemetery and a school. A mere total of 32 acres was surveyed for cultivation; and subsequently allocated as short-term leases to: -

Mary Andrews – 6 acres; Tom & Mary Nichols – 7 acres; William Nichols – 2 acres; Nathan Thompson – 3 acres; Isaac Mosely – 2 acres; Perry Johnson – 2 acres; Mary Field – 2 acres; Campbell Stevens – 2 acres; Ned King – 4 acres; John Robbins – 2 acres.

The leases, although granted, were of doubtful legality because the Crown Lands Act (and subsequent Lands Acts) failed to mention Lord Howe Island in its provisions. The seeds of mistrust were growing.

In 1881 the Government granted licence to an Auckland Company, Henderson & Macfarland, to collect guano from the Admiralty Islands for shipment to New Zealand. Charles Ponder was appointed as agent for the industry, which Armstrong hoped would give employment to the Islanders; as well as provide them with a regular shipping service for their market produce. However, instead of managing his bird manure, Ponder had his own agenda. In defiance of Armstrong's orders he began clearing large patches of land for his own cultivation, destroying many palms and other indigenous flora in the process. Armstrong wrote of Ponder:

I had to prevent by threatening him with the course of the Law and reported him to the government. In the meantime I had received communication from Noumea inquiring as to this very man, who was an absconding debtor from that place, and warning me of his general character. On his knowing I had become possessed of this knowledge he appears to have set zealously to work to destroy my influence, and by every form of annoyance to me endeavour to irritate me and bring my office into contempt.

With knowledge of Ponder's dubious background, Armstrong succeeded in having him removed from the Island and replaced by a man named Grimshaw. But the damage was done. Ponder had whispered into the ears of an already divided community, further undermining Armstrong's position on the Island.

Messrs Tapsell, Cameron and Cresswell landed from the schooner *Levuka* on 7 December 1881. They negotiated the first purchase of a large quantity of Kentia palm seeds with Armstrong. However, the Islanders considered these negotiations favoured Armstrong and were not in the community's best interest. This was the catalyst that led to a number of Islanders finally petitioning the NSW Government to recall Captain Armstrong.

The petition, bearing the names of fifteen adults plus several children, was lodged in December 1881 but was rejected by the Government. However, when Armstrong visited Sydney in January 1882, Charles Moore, Director of the Botanical Gardens, accused him of embezzling £30 paid for the supply of seeds. After a hasty investigation by Edmund Frosbery, the Inspector General of Police, the charge was upheld. Further, the Department of Public Instruction complained that he refused to account for money provided to build a school on the Island. These claims prompted the Government to review the Islanders' petition. Subsequently, an Inquiry was ordered into Armstrong's administration– an Inquiry that would be fraught with truths, half-truths, contradictions and innuendoes.

The Honourable John Bowie Wilson was appointed Commissioner for the Inquiry, arriving at the Island on *Thetis* on 4 April 1882.

Born in Scotland in 1820, John Bowie Wilson came to Australia in 1840 and settled in the Monaro district. Several years later he went back to Scotland for a short time, before moving to America. There he worked as an assistant to his brother who was a medical practitioner. Returning to Australia in 1854 he turned his hand to gold prospecting, and practiced as a doctor of hydropathy, before entering Parliament.

His service as a member of the NSW Legislative Assembly spanned thirteen years from 1859 to 1872. During that time he was member for Goldfields South, Patricks Plains, and finally East Sydney. He also held the post of Secretary for Lands on three occasions during his political career. A staunch liberal, John Bowie Wilson was the first president of the Liberal Association of New South Wales. Upon his political defeat in 1872 he became a stock, station and land agent, and was engaged in these activities at the time of his appointment to the Armstrong Inquiry.

Why John Bowie Wilson was appointed Commissioner for the Inquiry is unclear, as his only credentials were that he was a Justice of the Peace. He did not adjudicate any other case.

Prior to the proceedings, Captain Armstrong was suspended from duty. Two Islanders, John Robbins and Campbell Stevens, were appointed as Special Constables to seize all Government property held by him.

Of the seven charges brought against Armstrong by the Islanders, the Commissioner found *strong presumptive truth but not enough conclusive evidence* on four counts. His findings on the three other charges were: -

Charge 1: Neglecting to prosecute the charge made against one of his Kanaka workmen for criminal assault on a girl of tender years.

> This charge appears to be well substantiated. Although the father of the girl has given Captain Armstrong a letter to the effect that he was drunk at the time of laying the charge and now did not believe it, it must be borne in mind that the father was in Captain Armstrong's employment and an inmate of his house. It conveys to me a strong impression that it is an attempt to hush the matter up. A statement of the two women who were called in to see the girl was in evidence.

Charge 2: Attempting to monopolise the Island trade.

> The evidence I have been able to collect bears out this charge – namely, the attempt of Captain Armstrong to monopolise the trade of the Island. Even if the charge is too strongly put the very fact of his opening a store and exporting on his own account the natural products of the Island, shows that he has placed himself in direct antagonism with the inhabitants instead of having stimulated their exertions. It also underrates his want of appreciation of the dignity and responsibility of his office as paid Resident Magistrate.

Charge 3: Selling intoxicating drink to the inhabitants or in other words illegal grog selling.

This was the most serious charge and Commissioner Wilson found the *evidence of the truth of the charge overwhelming*, tabling Armstrong's alcohol accounts for Henry Wilson, John Robbins and Tom Nichols.

While Armstrong did not deny supplying the Islanders with intoxicating liquor, he said the total value did not exceed £20 in his three years as Resident Magistrate. His answer to the charge was in itself 'overwhelming':-

Finding on my arrival at the Island, more than three years ago, that several of the Islanders were distilling a rough, fiery spirit from the banana and wild figs, I remonstrated with them, and was instrumental in checking the evil. On occasions, too, when vessels touched at the Island a large portion of the produce was bartered by some of the Islanders for spirits, and little work was done until the stock thus procured was exhausted.

Seeing these evils, I let the inhabitants know that in cases of sickness, or necessity I would be prepared to give a little from my own private stock. This I did to remove what I thought the chief incentive to their laying in a stock; to cement a friendly feeling towards myself, and to gradually bring about a better tone of feeling among the people. At first this took the form of my giving the Islanders a glass of colonial wine on their calling at my house, or a bottle of wine in case of reported necessity in their families. This was sometimes reciprocated by a present of a bunch of bananas or some other produce of the Island.

Anxious as I was to serve the needs of the people, I soon found that I could not afford to supply them gratuitously, and wishing to keep in check the practice of applying for wine, and desirous of not encouraging the spirit of pauperism, I let it be known that any supplied must be represented by such produce as they might have for disposal, or by labour I might require at their hands. It was this that led to the keeping an exact account of all that was supplied. The very three accounts referred to in your Commissioner's Report represent supplies furnished to three families suffering from illness as I judged at the time, and was represented to me, mainly caused by low, poor diet.

In the case of H. Wilson, he represented that himself and the family he lived with, viz., Mosely and wife, were suffering from poorness of blood, which I thought would be removed or mitigated by a gentle stimulant in the shape of wine; the account of this man for wine amounts, I believe, to about £1 during three years, which is not yet settled.

In the case of Robbins, I may state that his wife had been nearly three months thoroughly prostrated with rheumatic fever, followed by a very difficult and dangerous confinement. I enquired into the case and at the earnest solicitations of her husband, allowed him to have the brandy, having from time to time given him (without charge) several bottles of wine.

In the case of T. Nichols, for a long time the wife had also suffered from rheumatic fever, general prostration, and debility. The children too (a numerous family) were weak and ill, and Nichols represented to me that a slight stimulant was absolutely necessary in their case, and informed me that he added a little wine to their porridge, finding it very beneficial.

I may here solemnly state that I have never known a solitary instance where any excess has followed from wine or spirits supplied from my stock; neither have I been called upon or seen the necessity during my administration to take any public action to check the use of stimulants, except in the case of the man Nichols, whom I declined to allow to have any more nearly six months ago.

In defence of his actions pertaining to the sale of alcohol, Armstrong told the Commissioner that the Island lacked essential medicines, and his requests for supplies had been constantly refused. To support this, he tabled a letter from the Government that quoted: -

It did not feel called upon to supply medicine for the people on the Island.

The Commissioner's finding in respect of the charge of running a sly grog shop was really quite absurd, considering that he and the official party that accompanied him to the Island had brought a quantity of wines, spirits and ales – all courtesy of the Government! Within a few days of their arrival, their campsite was strewn with empty bottles. When Armstrong asked Commissioner Wilson why he was drinking liquor, when he professed to be a teetotaller, the Commissioner angrily replied that the liquor was for medicinal purposes as the local water disagreed with him!

Armstrong certainly had grounds for questioning the Commissioner, particularly since John Bowie Wilson had been elected both President of the Excelsior Division of the Order of the Sons of Temperance in 1868, and Executive Member of the NSW Alliance for Suppression of Intemperance in 1869.

Not to be outdone the Commissioner found that a memo submitted by Armstrong, marked private, official and confidential, had blackened and slandered every petitioner who had signed the original complaint. And despite labelling Tom Nichols, the lead petitioner, as a heavy drinker, Armstrong had still supplied him with 60 bottles of wine and 12 bottles of brandy.

Many of the accusations in his memo were aimed at Thomas and Mary Nichols, and included: -

Mrs. T. Nichols was a very vindictive woman who proclaimed loudly against any interference of authority. She also compromised her reputation with a whaling captain whilst her husband was away at sea.

Commissioner Wilson's Camp (1882)

Photo Government Printer

Thomas Nichols, a lazy troublesome fellow – a sea lawyer who drank heavily – deliberately wrecked a ship in Noumea.

He did not see the necessity of authority and claimed the Island as his birthright declaring that the Government had no right to disturb them.

Indeed, Armstrong's allegation that Thomas Nichols deliberately wrecked a ship in Noumea was true. Attached to his report was the following letter from John Bell, dated 14 January 1880: -

I employed Thomas Nichols in the year 1878 as master of the barque Australasian Packet, for the purpose of procuring beche-de-mer. Campbell Stevens was also employed as mate. The crew, except for Stevens, later reported to me that Nichols, on leaving Sydney, took the vessel to Lord Howe Island and stayed there for several weeks during which time he took a large quantity of the ships stores, to which he had no right, to his house. The vessel was later wrecked, solely through Nichols' continued intemperance, and the wreck and ship's boats sold by him to traders in Noumea. He has neither written to me nor accounted in any way for the loss or sale of the wreck, and everything connected with the affair has been most mysterious and unsatisfactory. I had purposed at the time taking out a warrant against him, but in consequence of the great difficulties in the way of getting to him (at Lord Howe Island) and the extra expense I would have been put to, I was advised to withhold my prosecution. The vessel and trade was uninsured, and I lost over £6000 in the transaction.

The Armstrong Inquiry finished on 17 April 1882. The Commissioner's Report was handed to the Colonial Secretary on 19 May with the following recommendation:-

After careful consideration of the whole case, I am decidedly of opinion that a Resident Magistrate is not required at Lord Howe Island, and that the inhabitants generally do not require one; and considering the serious nature of the charges against Captain Armstrong, I recommend that his suspension be confirmed.

On 31 May 1882 Armstrong was removed from Public Service and his official appointments terminated. Further, on John Bowie Wilson's recommendations, the guano industry ceased. Grimshaw, his labourers, and Armstrong's employees departed the Island. However, Armstrong was permitted to return in December that year to view the Transit of Venus.

The scientific survey team preparing for this event arrived on the Island with John Bowie Wilson in April 1882. It was during this time that the first photographs of Lord Howe Island were taken. The Transit of Venus was observed on 8 December from a hill called Lookout Mound, known today as Transit Hill. While on this visit several scientists, and the deposed Captain Armstrong, made the first landing on Balls Pyramid.

Upon Armstrong's dismissal, Campbell Stevens was appointed Forest Ranger and Postmaster. He held the former position until 1891 but continued as Postmaster for another thirty-three years. He moved from North Bay, settling on a portion of the 100 acres previously held by Armstrong, known now as Stevens Reserve. He and John Robbins retained their positions as Special Constables even though three days after their appointment by John Bowie Wilson, they were accused of breaking into the schoolhouse!

The Armstrong Inquiry may have officially ended, but the controversy surrounding it was only just beginning

With his honour and reputation sullied, Armstrong vigorously appealed with a campaign of letters to the Press and representations to the Government. He published a pamphlet titled *The Removal of Captain Armstrong from Government Service*, in which he complained that only those nine Islanders who were against his administration had been called to give evidence. They were neither cautioned to tell the truth, nor was he permitted to cross-examine them.

Several new petitions, objecting to Armstrong's dismissal, were signed by *three-quarters of the Island's most respectable inhabitants* and sent to the Legislative Assembly and Council. The petitioners deemed the charge of sly-grog selling as frivolous and absurd. One petition stated: -

> In the seven months since his departure there have been more disturbances, complaints and unfriendly feeling among the people than ever occurred during the whole of his reign here.

How the demeanour of the Islanders must have changed since the visit by Surgeon Corrie in 1876 when he wrote: -

> Bickerings and open quarrels are unusual and distasteful. Disputed questions are generally referred to a retired American whaling captain (Nathan Thompson) and thus settled amongst themselves

The new petitions were dismissed with the Government taking the view that *every man from statesman to stablehand firmly believes that his own friends and supporters are the most respectable of people*. It also noted that several names on the new petitions had appeared on the original document requesting Armstrong's removal and, according to his memo at the time, they were definitely not the most respectable citizens. Four illiterate persons supporting Armstrong denied having put their mark on the first petition. It was later claimed the writing of their names on that document bore an uncanny resemblance to the handwriting of Captain Tom Nichols!

Ironically, Armstrong had a strong ally in Albert, the literate 18 year-old son of Tom and Mary Nichols. Albert sent a letter supporting Armstrong's case against his parents, in which he stated: -

> Hearing of certain accusations made by them, I consider you have been most grossly maligned, and I now wish, out of justice to you, to make this statement, that on every occasion I have been sent by my parents to you for wine or spirits that they have told me to ask for it medicinally, on account of illness in the family – more especially by my father. I also know that on occasions you have lent them money, especially when they wanted to send me to Sydney, and they promised in my presence, to return the loan in a few days, which I am convinced they did not do, as you had to take out the value in produce from our homestead at our own prices, though such produce was almost valueless to us.
>
> I may state that I have never known you to act in any way but most gentlemanly and honourably towards us all on the Island; and you have at all times given us the very best advice and counsel, especially to the young people, while your manner has always been kind and considerate to all.
>
> I regret to say that I am perfectly ashamed of the conduct of my parents of late towards you.

Needless to say, Albert left the Island soon after his letter was made public. He did not return. In an affidavit before James Farnell JP, Albert declared that his mother, in an act of violence, had struck him with a spade and threatened to shoot him for his betrayal. From the wrath of his mother on Lord Howe Island, to the wrath of Mother Nature in the North Atlantic – thirty years later Albert would lose his life as boatswain on the *Titanic*.

In February 1883 general agitation prompted the appointment of a Select Parliamentary Committee to reassess the Commissioner's findings. This Committee condemned Wilson's methods, questioned the character of the accusers, and virtually cleared Armstrong, apart from a mild rebuke for supplying liquor. However, the bias of

Albert Nichols

this Committee was as obvious as that shown by the Commissioner during the Inquiry, and the report was received with some scepticism. To make matters worse, John Bowie Wilson died before the report was submitted for the Legislative Assembly's decision. The ruling was delayed out of respect for his memory.

The Government, seeking peace with honour, offered Armstrong alternate employment. But, already aroused by what he considered a manifest injustice, Armstrong preferred to seek public vindication by compensation. This led him to publish a second pamphlet, titled *Captain Armstrong R.N. re Lord Howe Island*. In June 1884 a new Select Committee recommended £1000 compensation but strong opposition from Sir John Robertson, a friend of John Bowie Wilson, delayed settlement. Armstrong published yet another pamphlet, titled *Captain Armstrong, R.N. and Sir John Robertson*.

On 20 April 1886 his case was expounded at the bar of the House by his counsel David Buchanan. But on 18 June a motion for £3000 compensation was rejected as being excessive. However in April 1887, five years after the Inquiry, his protagonists reluctantly agreed to a compromise offer of £1500. Captain Armstrong was finally compensated and his honour and dignity were upheld.

The newspapers of the day supported Armstrong, with the editor of the *Evening News* reporting: -

> Whether the Captain is guilty or not does not matter in the least; he has not been tried. If we had not the Select Committee report for authority, it would be almost impossible to believe that anywhere in the British dominions, even on a rock in the Pacific, a man could be tried, found guilty, sentenced, and punished without being allowed to call a witness on his behalf, or to open his mouth in his own defence. The thing is so monstrous as to be almost incredible.

Among the many documents Armstrong published relating to the case was a letter from an acquaintance who said he had met Commissioner Wilson. The acquaintance claimed the Commissioner had told him that the Government had nothing against Armstrong – it merely wanted to abolish the post of Administrator on the Island. He further claimed that Wilson's trip, which coincided with the survey for the Transit of Venus, was just a pleasure jaunt; and a blind for the Government's intention to bring Armstrong home. Conveniently, the letter was not published until after John Bowie Wilson's death.

Captain Armstrong did not return to the Island. He used his compensation money in farming ventures in New South Wales, and later moved to Tasmania where he volunteered for service in the Boer War. In 1902, he moved to Western Australia, where he pioneered sponge fisheries. He died in Perth in 1910 at the age of 79.

Who really gained from the Armstrong affair? A summation of the Inquiry at the time quoted the following: -

> The Lord Howe Island case was a cause célèbre which aroused all the liberals in New South Wales including Sir Alfred Stephen. Armstrong was probably guilty of at least serious indiscretion and but for Wilson's extraordinary procedure would have received little support. Bowie Wilson who was near to death and influenced by Charles Moore, saw the case not as an inquiry but a crusade against immorality. His friends sought to protect his memory; Armstrong's party sought to assert his right to natural justice; the island beachcombers sought only the removal of interfering authority and succeeded.

Or did they? On John Bowie Wilson's recommendation, Lord Howe Island was supervised by a succession of visiting magistrates until 1913. That year, the NSW Government formed a Sydney-based Board of Control for the Island. Members visited on a yearly basis until 1940 when, 58 years after the Armstrong Inquiry, a resident superintendent was again appointed. By coincidence, less than twelve months after his appointment, that administrator was also removed. He was taken back to the mainland in a straitjacket! A succession of administrators has since been appointed from various Government departments.

13

THE JEUNE AFFAIR

Edmund Jeune settled on Lord Howe Island with his wife and children in March 1889. Shortly after his arrival, he entered into partnership with Perry Johnson, conditions of which were detailed in a written agreement signed by both parties. Edmund was permitted to erect a dwelling on Perry's property and, in consideration for working the gardens and performing other duties, he was to receive a third of all remuneration from the sale of produce. However, by January 1890 the partnership had dissolved into a nasty dispute over forty bunches of bananas. Both parties accused the other of breaching the agreement. The incident caused a judicial inquiry that pitted Islanders against each other.

Edmund claimed he had not been paid for his share of the profit from the bananas, which had been shipped to the Sydney market. Perry counter-claimed that the bananas, planted before the partnership commenced, had not been picked by Edmund and therefore he was not entitled to a share. Perry also accused Edmund of lying about his marital status, as the real Mrs Jeune was in the process of divorcing him on the gounds of his adultery with Celine. According to Perry, Edmund's dishonesty was further evident when he failed to inform him of a serious heart condition, which affected his ability to undertake manual work on the farm.

The matter was heard before the visiting Magistrate, Thomas Icely, and the two special constables, Campbell Stevens and John Robbins. Citing a copy of the stamped agreement, which had been drawn up and witnessed by Tom Nichols, the magistrate ruled against Edmund Jeune. Mr Icely found him to be a *mean and contemptible man who had seduced a young girl while he was still married.*

Celine Moore had applied for the teacher's position under the name of Jeune. Her application was rejected on the grounds that she was not married to Edmund. In begging for justice from Magistrate Icely, Celine said she was proud to be that *young* girl, and at 34 years of age had lived with Edmund Jeune for four years. She argued that no man could be a kinder husband or better father to their two children; and as soon as his divorce was finalised they intended to legalise their union. Celine pleaded that due to the dispute over the bananas, and Edmund's heart disease, they were penniless and depended on the generosity of several Islanders for their survival.

A letter of support for Edmund Jeune was submitted, stating: -

We the undersigned residents of Lord Howe Island, desire to place on record our sympathy with you in the matter of the case lately brought before the Visiting Justice (T. R. Icely, Esq.) who, without reference to the case under consideration, made certain observations regarding your character, with which we entirely disagree, for you have, during your stay among us, gained our respect as a man and parent. And we assure you that these accusations shall not be the means of alienating our respect from – and knowing the disease from which you suffer, we trust that you may long be spared to us as a friend.

> (Signed) T.B. Wilson, Nathan Thompson, William Thompson,
> Daniel Hamill, Ned King, Patrick Mooney

Edmund Jeune was not spared. A broken man, he and his family departed in April 1890. However, several months later they tried to return when Celine once again unsuccessfully applied for the teaching position.

At the time of the proceedings against Jeune, W E Langley, Registrar of Births, Deaths & Marriages, was having problems of his own. He had evidence of a conspiracy by some residents to have him removed from the Island, and asked Mr Icely to bring the conspirators to justice. When the Magistrate refused to act Langley complained to the Government, demanding an inquiry into the general conduct of judicial proceedings on the Island. He claimed the ruling in the Jeune case was influenced by the friendship between the Magistrate, his judicial panel and Perry Johnson and was therefore an example of a gross miscarriage of justice.

There was no inquiry. Magistrate Icely justified his method of conducting proceedings on the Island, stating: -

> While I adhere to State Books of the Colony I need the ability to use a large amount of discretion to the largely small matters, which are not best served by normal formalities given the unusual land tenure/laws etc. that exist on the Island and the small nature of the community. I wish to act in less formal ways, in most instances and reduce costs to Islanders with regards to proceedings and thus ensure I am more available to them.

After the complaint was dismissed, Magistrate Icely asked the Government to terminate Langley's position and remove him from the Island. However, his request was also denied and Mr Langley remained at his post until his death in 1894. Shortly after the Jeune inquiry, Mr Brodie replaced Icely as the visiting Magistrate.

14

TWO FAMILIES - SEVEN GENERATIONS

The Island is full of families - and not many of them – (Mick Nichols, 1985)

By the turn of the 20th century, the offspring of Lord Howe Island's first permanent settlers – Thomas and Margaret Andrews and Nathan and Bokue Thompson – were producing a fourth generation of Islanders.

Interestingly, a part genealogical trace of the Thompson and Nichols lineages to 16th and 19th century England found the name Chase common to both families. Although not of the same direct line, perhaps further back in medieval England, Chase could have been a common denominator connecting the two families.

Most of the early residents spent their entire lives on the Island. However, as the 20th century progressed, educational and career opportunities became priorities with many families. Consequently many young Islanders moved to the mainland. But, with the Island forever in their blood some stayed only a short time, while others returned upon retiring from their chosen careers. Of course there were many who did not return. Marrying and raising families on the mainland and abroad, seventh generation descendants of the original families now live in Australia, England, Wales and the USA.

In the winter of 2005 the population of Lord Howe Island totalled 363, including children attending mainland schools. This number excluded residents who had moved to the mainland for indefinite periods. A breakdown of the total is as follows: -

- 148 lineal descendants from the original families:
  134 descended from Thompson
  25 descended from Andrews
  (17 of these 159 share both Andrews and Thompson lineage)
  4 descended from Fenton
  (2 of these 4 share Fenton and Thompson lineage
  1 descended from Baxter.
- 57 persons are spouses/partners of the lineal descendants.
- 67 persons are individuals of over 10-year residency.
- 91 persons are public servants, hospital staff, teachers and others employed on the Island on short term contracts.

Included in the 363 total are fourteen seventh generation descendants from the Andrews and Thompsons. James and Alana Green are seventh generation from both lines: -

Thomas-Margaret Andrews   Nathan-Bokue Thompson
Mary Andrews-Tom Nichols   Mary Thompson-T B Wilson
Grace Nichols-Hector Innes   Mabel Wilson-Henry Payten
Margaret Innes-Frank Payten
Jean Payten-Horace Green
John Green-Vicki Green
James and Alana

ANDREWS/NICHOLS LINE

Thomas Andrews-Margaret (Curry)

Margaret Curry was born in 1813 in County Waterford, Ireland, to George Curry and Mary Chatford. In 1832 Margaret immigrated to Australia on the ship *James Paterson*. On arriving in Sydney, she gained employment as Upper Housemaid to the wife of a stationer in George Street. During the voyage from England, Margaret met Thomas Andrews, a Second Mate on the emigrant ship. A romance blossomed and they were married in St. Philip's Church, Sydney, in 1836.

After their marriage, the Sydney Harbourmaster employed Thomas to moor the first floating lightship at the Sow and Pigs where the couple lived as lightkeepers for nine months. Thomas then purchased a small lighter of about 12 tons, which was chartered as a freight carrier for Walker's and Moore's Wharves in Sydney Harbour. However, in 1842 a slump in business forced him to sell the lighter. At that time Captain Sheridan, an old shipmate of Thomas, was in command of *Rover's Bride*. He introduced Thomas and Margaret to Captain Poole who immediately offered them twelve months employment on Lord Howe Island.

After completing their term Thomas and Margaret returned to the mainland, where they purchased 400 acres of land for farming. However, the depression of the early 1840s, described in an 1890 statement by Margaret as *the great insolvency bringing ruin and disaster to thousands*, forced them to sell the land less than a year later for just £10. Today, that land encompasses North Sydney Railway Station.

Captain Poole then employed them for another term; and this time they made Lord Howe Island their home. Their daughter, Mary, was born in 1846.

Thomas died in 1860. Margaret died in 1891. They were buried in the family cemetery that was later officially recognised as Pinetrees cemetery.

Thomas Nichols-Mary (Andrews)

William Chase emigrated from England to Australia in 1830. His daughters, Anne and Caroline, and their mother Sarah Brooks, followed as assisted immigrants on the *Strathfieldsay* in 1834. After settling in Tasmania, William and Sarah were married. In 1837 Anne, then 19 years of age, married Thomas Arnold Nichols, a Master on Colonial ships. Their son, Thomas George, was born in Hobart on 5 May 1838. The family moved to Victoria for a time where another son was born but Anne died shortly after. William's second marriage to Anne Priest produced William jnr, who in 1862, accompanied his half-brother Thomas to the Island. A month after their arrival, Thomas married Mary Andrews.

Thomas died on the Island in 1897. As a Master Mason of the Tasmanian Operative Lodge, which he joined in 1859, his headstone bears the Masonic symbol. Mary died in Sydney in 1923. She was buried in Sutherland Cemetery.

Albert, born in 1864, left the Island after the Armstrong Inquiry, never to return. Fearful for his life, he left on the steamer *Suva* on 7 August 1882. His planned departure, shrouded in secrecy, was known only to his youngest brother George, who was the only sibling he was able to farewell. Albert worked on a Sydney ferry and at night schooled himself to improve his education. His mother tried to have him brought back to the Island; but as he was 18 years of age, and earning an honest living, she could not legally force him to return.

Later, Albert found passage as seaman on a ship to England, where he married Jane Porter from Ayrshire in Scotland. They had two children, Thomas and Jean. Albert joined the White Star Line and became known within the Company as 'Big Neck'. He was boatswain on the *Olympic* before transferring to the *Titanic* in Belfast. When that ship berthed in Southampton, he was on the crew list for her maiden voyage to New York. On 15 April 1912, Albert was one of the 1523 souls who perished in one of the world's greatest ocean tragedies. He was last seen taking six crew members to open lower gangway doors in a desperate bid to save steerage passengers. Perhaps aware of his fate, he gave his whistle to a passenger in a lifeboat requesting that it be returned to his family in Southampton. The whistle is still in the possession of Albert's descendants today.

Charles, third son of Tom and Mary was born in 1867. He left the Island with his wife and son, Osborne Wright, in 1900. Amelia died shortly after while singing in the choir of the church in which they were married. She was just 34 years of age and pregnant with their second child. Osborne, an epileptic, died on the mainland of a cerebral haemorrhage in 1925 at the age of 27. Charles periodically visited the Island until he married again in 1907. That marriage produced four children and upon the early death of his second wife, he married yet again. That union produced another four children. Charles died in Sydney in 1941 aged 77.

Anne, the youngest of Tom and Mary's children, was born in 1886. Her parents treated her harshly and, when she was 18 years old, her siblings smuggled her onto a passing ship. Anne did not return. She married Jim Lawrence and had two children, Ken and Mary. The relationship with her mother must have improved over the years as Mary died while visiting Anne in Sydney in 1923. Anne died in 1978.

George (1869-1947), Mary (1871-1933), Grace (1874-1953), Edith (1879-1964), Martha (1881-1945) and Susan (1884-1968) remained on the Island. Like their father and grandparents they were buried in the family cemetery at Pinetrees. Many fifth and sixth generation children of Thomas and Margaret reside on the Island today. The lineal descent has reached the seventh generation through their granddaughters, Mary Challis and Grace.

At the time of this book going to print, Ashley Retmock had entered the world. Although he made his debut on the mainland, this little grandson of Dean and Linda Retmock, and great-great-great grandson of Mary Challis, is the first eighth generation descendant from the Andrews line. The seventh generation children before him are: -

Thomas-Margaret Andrews
Mary Andrews-Tom Nichols
Mary Nichols-William Retmock
Charles Retmock-Amelia Dignam
Bill Retmock-Doreen Browne

Lisa Retmock-Tangi Makiiti – Rod Oxley   Matthew Retmock-Suzy Gillette
Tamarua Makiiti and Sunny Oxley   Nelson and Nathan

 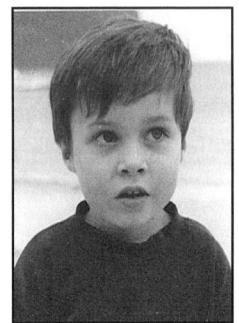  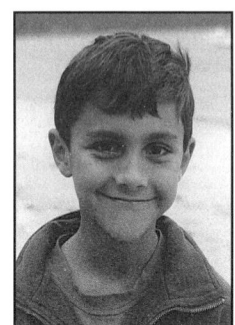

Thomas-Margaret Andrews
Mary Andrews-Tom Nichols
Grace Nichols-Hector Innes
Alec Innes-Vera Dignam
Mavis Innes-Jim Fitzgerald
Ian Fitzgerald-Marie Andall
Bianca

Tamarua, Sunny, Nelson, Nathan and Bianca are also sixth generation descendants of Nathan and Bokue Thompson.

Nathan Chase was born to James Thompson and Peace Chase in 1823, in Somerset, a small town northwest of New Bedford, Massachusetts. His heritage can be traced back to the birth of William Chase in England in 1595. Married to Mary Townley, he sailed to America on the *Arbella* in 1630 with John Winthrop, the appointed Governor of the Massachusetts Bay colony. In 1638 William and his family settled at Yarmouth on Cape Cod, where he was appointed Constable the following year. Ironically, he was later removed from that position for selling alcohol.

William's son and then a grandson, born in 1645, were also named William. The latter married Hannah Herman and had a son Isaac, year of birth unknown. Isaac married Mary Fowler to whom Ezekiel was born in 1723. Ezckicl's marriage to Elizabeth Buffington produced Ezra in 1745. Ezra married his cousin Peace Chase and their daughter, named after her mother, was born in 1780. Peace married her cousin James Thompson.

Among William Chase's descendants was whaler Owen Chase who was mate on the *Essex* when that ship was stove by a whale in 1820. The tragedy and events that followed, which included cannibalism in a long fight for survival on the open sea, were the inspiration for Herman Melville's epic 1851 novel, *Moby Dick*.

The third generation William, born in 1645, and his brother John were the respective great-great-great grandfathers of Nathan Thompson and Owen Chase.

On 12 July 1845 Nathan signed on as boatsteerer on the barque *Pacific*; sailing out of New Bedford. After reaching Sydney in October 1847 he deserted the ship and joined the *Belle*. However, according to a crew list for September 1852 Nathan had deserted that ship some months before at Pell's Island, 905 nautical miles northwest of Honolulu. It is not known what ship he sailed on to reach the Gilbert Islands but it was there that he rejoined the *Belle*. While whaling within these islands, Nathan and two shipmates rescued Boranga, Bogaroo and Bokue – natives adrift in a canoe off the island of Abemama. Rather than leave them to an unknown fate in the sea, they took the castaways on the *Belle* but were forced to disembark with them after it reached Lord Howe Island.

Bokue, the daughter of a tribal chief, had refused to marry a much older man – a brave decision for a girl of 14 to make in a time and place where such marriages were customary. In 1982 three great-grandchildren of Nathan and Bokue – Betty Elliot, Bruce and Michael Thompson – travelled to Kiribati for the purpose of tracing Bokue's ancestry. In the main island of Tarawa, they managed to find whaling records of visiting ships including several trips made by the *Belle*. However, written genealogical records, if any existed, were destroyed or lost during the Japanese invasion in World War II. On learning that ancestral lineage was passed by word of mouth from generation to generation, they spoke with elders of various families. Although they failed to find a family link, they learned that in Bokue's era punishment for not complying with the laws of tribal marriage was, indeed, to be cast to sea, to either die or perchance on the sanctuary of another island. Boranga and Bogaroo would have been her handmaidens, from a lesser class within her tribe.

Nathan died in 1895. Bokue died in 1897. Both were buried in the Thompson cemetery located on a portion of their land.

Nathan and Bokue's children – Mary (1866-1943), William (1868-1953), Emeline (1870-1952), Rosario (1871-1956) and John (1878-1963) spent their lives on the Island and were buried in the family cemetery.

A large proportion of Islanders are descended from Nathan and Bokue and today a number of children are seventh generation: -

Nathan-Bokue Thompson
Mary Thompson-Thomas Bryant Wilson
Gower Wilson-Ada Austic

Roy Wilson-Daphne Rundell   Allen Wilson-Eve Smyth
Judy Wilson-Peter Riddle   Kevin Wilson-Sue Sewell
Amy Riddle-Luke Hickey   KellyWilson-Keith Galloway
Wilson   Ryan

Nathan-Bokue Thompson
Mary Thompson-Thomas Bryant Wilson
Elsie Wilson-Harry Smythe
Dawn Smythe-John Young
Brian Young-Annette Wilson

Daniel Young-Andrea Calf   Jozette Young-Utia Makiiti
Taylah and Marnie   Seanna

Nathan-Bokue Thompson
John Thompson-Isabella Hansen
Daisy Thompson -Harry Woolnough
Betty Woolnough-Alistair Crombie

Denise Crombie-Brian Ellis   Gary Crombie-JulieBretnall
Michelle Ellis-Geoffrey Thompson   Emma Crombie-Darren Nobbs
Damian   Mitchell

   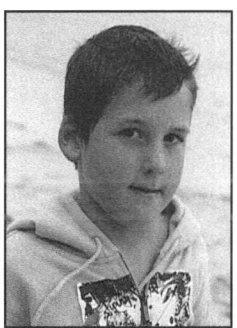

James, Alana, Taylah, Marnie, Sienna, Wilson, Ryan, Damian and Mitchell are 14th
generation descendants of William and Mary Chase from 16th century England.

THE PALM SEED INDUSTRY

Seeding

In the late 1870s, a revival of Lord Howe Island's economy emerged in the form of an endemic plant – the beautiful Kentia palm. Although distinct from the true 'Kentia' palm of New Guinea the name has been kept, and botanists have added the name Howea, in honour of its Island home.

The Island boasts four palm species, two of which prefer the moist conditions of Mount Gower and Mount Lidgbird. The Big Mountain palm (Hedyscepe canterburyana) is found upward from an elevation of about 350 m, while the Little Mountain palm (Lepidorrhachis mooreana) is restricted to the summits. The Kentia palm (Howea forsteriana) and the Curly palm (Howea belmoreana), tolerant to conditions in cool temperate climates unsuited to tropical palms, thrive along the lowlands.

Long before its entry into the world of commerce, the Kentia palm served the early Islanders well. Known locally as the Thatch palm, the tough leaves provided thatching for the roofs and walls of their homes. Battens split from the trunks were fastened over the thatching to prevent it being blown away in summer cyclones and winter gales. Even when more substantial timber dwellings were being built, palm thatch was still used in boatsheds and outbuildings until the 1940s.

For many years palm leaves were woven into baskets that were used to carry farm produce, or suspended from rafters to keep vegetables out of reach of marauding rats and mice. Decorative baskets were also popular with visitors. During the flying boat era, tourists often departed the Island with palm baskets interlaced with hibiscus and frangipani.

The mat of stringy fibre that protects the growing heart of a palm also provided early Islanders with many uses – tinder for fires, mattress and pillow stuffing, and protective packing for farm produce shipped to the mainland. With no such luxury as petal soft toilet paper, the fibre was also a prerequisite for Island toilets. At first the loos were just timber planks, with a hole cut in the centre, which were strategically placed over the spreading trunks of banyan trees. Later, outside shelters were constructed housing pits that were known as 'the long drops'.

The first exporter of palm seed from the Island was Ned King, who was a mountain guide for Surveyor Fitzgerald's scientific visits in 1869 and 1876. At the request of the Botanical Gardens he supplied them with palm seeds, seedlings and other native plants. The inscription on the stencil plate for his seed bag, read: -

E. King, the oldest established seed and plant merchant in Lord Howe Island

T B Wilson pioneered the first overseas market in 1880, followed by Mary Nichols and William Nichols, who by 1884, were selling seeds to Belgium, England, America and India.

By the end of the 1880s, Europe was the biggest single customer for the burgeoning palm seed industry. In 1894 the Kentia palm attracted the interest of the Sydney-based horticultural company Searles, who sent their landscape architect Alexander Fenton to the Island to procure both seeds and seedlings for the Australian market.

Although trading markets had been established, the development of the industry was haphazard, offering little benefit to the Islanders who were continually undercutting each other in price. Sydney seed merchants took advantage of the situation, at times paying Islanders only 2/6d per bushel when the going rate on the mainland was as high as 10/- and in England as high as £3. Often the Islanders were not paid in cash but in goods that were given an inflated value by the middlemen (mostly Sydney seedsmen). There were occasions when they were not paid at all and were forced to replace so-called defective seed, incurring the shipping costs as well.

In 1904 the visiting magistrate Frank Farnell, mindful of the Islanders' plight and lack of business acumen, obtained a Permissive Occupancy over the unoccupied Crown Lands for the purpose of extending the seed industry. He offered his services as a broker (with no commission) to the eight principal seeders/exporters, in order to increase the price and ensure full payment for seeds. He hoped this would give some measure of control to the Islanders. An agreement was reached on 1 January 1905. The eight exporters were Mary Nichols, George Nichols, T B Wilson, William Thompson, Phillip Dignam, Alexander Fenton, John Robbins and George Waterhouse.

Towards the end of 1905 an English seed company, Sander & Son, entered into negotiations with Farnell. Their proposal was to purchase no less than 750 bushel of seed per annum for a period of seven years at 8/- per thousand seeds for the first two years, and 10/- per thousand for the following five years. However, Australian nurserymen protested to the Chief Secretary, as such an agreement would have given Sander & Son a monopoly on the industry. The State Government ultimately blocked the proposal.

A significant development took place in July 1906 when Frank Farnell formed the Kentia Palm Seed and Plant Cooperative Ltd, in conjunction with twenty-one Islanders and a Sydney based seed business, Horton & Company. Frank Farnell was appointed Chairman of Directors with George Nichols as Island Director.

Of the 2400 shares in the Cooperative, 1690 "A" shares were allocated to the Island shareholders. They divided their allotment into parcels of 135, 50 and 25 – based on the interest each shareholder held in the industry at the time the Company was formed. Fifty "A" shares were distributed between Frank Farnell and the Company's solicitor, William Shipway. The remaining 660 "B" shares were allotted to C J Symonds, seed merchant and owner of Horton & Company. As the major shareholder he acquired sole right to appoint an agent for the Kentia Company and duly appointed his own business, which was managed by his brother, E Symonds.

With a paid up capital of £2400, and a selling price for the seeds fixed at £2 per bushel f.o.b. (free on board) at Lord Howe Island, the Kentia Cooperative was in business.

The seeding season began in March each year and continued throughout winter into early spring. Collecting seeds was by no means an easy task, and even today it is suited only to the strong and able. The seeder used a circular strap, often made of layered hessian, to grip the trunk with his feet, then jack-knifed his way to the top of the palm. Wrenching the seed spikes from under the crown of palm leaves, he either tossed them to the ground or slung them over his arms as he slid back down the trunk. The seeds were then shelled from their spikes and packed into jute or hessian bags. Strapped onto a seeder's back in a specially constructed harness called a 'cubby', the bags were carried to waiting boats at nearby beaches or bays for delivery to the community seed shed at the jetty. There they were packed into moist earth to await shipment to the mainland.

The seeds were despatched to Sydney in bags containing two bushels (54 kgs) each. Delivery of orders to mainland buyers was made directly from the wharf, with the balance transferred to Horton & Company's store to be repacked for further shipment.

The demand for their produce saw the output of Kentia palm seeds increase annually with 1654, 1930 and 2302 bushels sold in 1908, 1909 and 1910 respectively.

However, trouble was again brewing in Paradise! As the industry expanded, the arbitrary division of profits created considerable jealousy and mistrust. Some shareholders became increasingly dissatisfied with the number of shares allocated to them, and non-shareholders claimed that because the profits were derived from Crown Lands they should be entitled to share in the benefits. There were also suspicions that Horton & Company was not paying the full returns entitled to the shareholders.

Consequently a special resolution was passed by the shareholders in late 1910. It permitted the issue of another 1200 shares to native-born Lord Howe Islanders who, at the age of 21, were bona fide residents. These shares carried no voting power, and would be forfeited to the Company upon the death of a shareholder. However, subject to the discretionary powers of the Directors, they could be reissued to the deceased's spouse and children.

Another condition of the resolution was that holders of the original "A" and "B" shares would be paid initially with dividends of 22/- and 36/- per share respectively. Only after they had received full payment would the deferred shareholders receive their dividends of 36/- per share. Likewise, "A" and "B" shareholders would then have to wait until after the deferred shareholders had been paid in full before they received any further dividends.

The resolution did little to allay the disquiet over the proportionate distribution of shares. In 1911 Hugh Langwell from the Western Land Board, and former member of the Legislative Assembly, was appointed to lead a Commission of Inquiry into the control of the Kentia palm seed trade.

It was only after Langwell's report, published on 26 April 1911, that the Islanders became fully aware of the financial operations of the Cooperative; and the manner in which their agent, Horton & Company, was conducting the business. Langwell found that an Australian Palm Seed Export Company had been formed shortly after the establishment of the Kentia Cooperative. The shareholders of this Company were Messrs Milner, Harries and C J Symonds – although his name did not appear on the share register. Milner and Harries were experienced seed men from London who were well acquainted with European buyers.

Symonds' positions as owner of Horton & Company and major shareholder in the Export Company created an obvious conflict of interest. Thus, the export trade through Horton & Company was not in the total interest of the Kentia Cooperative. At the time of the Commission in 1911, financial documents for the Australian Palm Seed Export Company had not been posted since April 1909.

The information collected by Langwell prompted another Royal Commission into the Kentia palm seed trade, and the welfare of the Islanders in general. It was held on the Island between 7 and 21 August 1912 and continued in Sydney until 5 November. This Commission, led by Walter Bevan, barrister-at-law, determined that the operations of the Kentia Company had resulted in much greater prosperity for the Islanders than had previously existed. Messrs Farnell and Shipway had received certain payments on account of dividends, but in every case the moneys were used for the benefit of Island shareholders, and they had not profited personally from the Kentia Company.

However, the Commission found that while Horton & Company had accounted for the total seed despatched from the Island, the agency had exercised too much control over the Kentia Company's affairs. At times, large sums of money had remained in Horton & Company's hands instead of being paid into the Kentia Company's bank account. The agency merely fed the Kentia Company as funds were required.

The Commission was unable to determine the true position of the Australian Palm Seed Export Company, as financial documents had still not been provided, and the Company's solvency was in doubt. Mr Milner had abandoned the Company in 1909 and had no idea of its operations since that time. Mr Harries, the only other listed shareholder who could account for the proceedings of the business, suddenly left for Europe when the Commission returned to Sydney to complete the Inquiry! There was no further mention made of C J Symonds.

Commissioner Bevan's recommendations regarding the palm industry included: -

- All permissive occupancies and all licences to collect palm seeds be cancelled.

- The Kentia Palm Company be wound up and its assets taken over by a new company.

- That a Board be immediately appointed to take charge of the affairs of the Island.

- That such a Board consists of three persons, to be appointed by the Government, to whom a permissive occupancy of the whole Island should be granted, and to whom authority should be given to collect and export seeds and palms.

- That the Board should appoint a certain number of Islanders to act as a local committee, to supervise the Island under its control, and an agent for the sale of palm seed and palms under such control condition as may be approved.

- That the Board form a Limited Liability Cooperative Company for the purpose of regulating and controlling the trade in palm seed.

Following these recommendations, the Lord Howe Island Board of Control was appointed on 27 February 1913. Shortly after, the Limited Liability Cooperative Company was formed and its first order of 312 bushels (8,424 kgs) of seed was shipped to Sydney on 19 March 1913. The new company allowed the original "A" shareholders to retain their shares, and determined the criteria for distribution of new £1 shares to all other Islanders.

When the men turned 21 they were entitled to 25 shares, which increased to 50 shares after ten years. When women turned 21 they were entitled to 10 shares, which increased to 25 shares only upon marriage to another shareholder. When children were born to shareholders, 10 shares were allotted for the upkeep of each child. However, when a male child reached the age of 21 and received his own entitlement, the 10-share upkeep payment was cancelled. The payment for females remained in place until they married. For economic reasons, some marriages on Lord Howe Island in that era were probably made in palm plantations – and not in Heaven!

As stated in the original 1906 agreement, no shareholder was allowed more than 135 shares. The only exception was Mary Nichols who, on the recommendation of the Royal Commission, retained 185 shares – 135 of her own "A" shares plus 50 shares given to her in 1909 by her son Charles, when he knew he would not return to the Island.

There were some peculiar conditions of the new Cooperative. One was that shareholders who left the Island for lengthy periods had to forfeit their shares. However, upon their return they could participate as shareholders again but only after completing a residency of two months for every year of absence from the Island. Another was that shareholders earning more than £24 per year from other sources, such as tourism, had a percentage of their shares deducted. All Islanders were expected to help harvest, cart, pack and ship seed under the direction of a three-man local committee appointed by the Board. Failure to comply with these rules meant the permanent loss of one's shares.

An additional wage was paid to those performing specific tasks relating to the seed industry. Dividends were paid on the shares at the end of every month.

A year after the Cooperative was formed the outbreak of World War I disrupted the European market. Seed was still harvested for the Australian market but in much reduced quantities. A further setback occurred in 1918, when the grounding of the *Makambo* led to a rat plague on the Island that almost decimated the industry.

With measures in place to try and combat the destruction by rats, palm seed export continued on a smaller scale through the 1920s and 1930s. Ironically, the world economic depression, beginning in 1929, had little impact on the industry because the Kentia palm was a luxury item and many of its buyers were not affected by conditions at the time. An article on Lord Howe Island's palm seed industry in an August 1936 edition of the Saturday Evening Post quoted: -

> There is something outrageously taking about the way this collectivist seed ship floats, buoyantly and defiantly, on the seething surface of the modern world.

During this period the Board of Control experimented with a small nursery, aiming to export seedlings rather than seed. However, in the late 1930s a decline in demand forced the Nursery's closure and a reduction in shareholders' payments.

When World War II broke out, the industry temporarily ceased. The share system collapsed and was not revived. Island families grew vegetable, fruit and flower seeds for mainland seed companies such as Yates and Rumseys. At the end of the War there was only a small market for palm seeds; and Islanders were paid a fixed sum of 6/- per bushel collected. All profits derived from the sale of seeds went into the Board's consolidated funds for Island administration.

The annual seed harvest remained at about 300 bushels for many years. Then in 1960, seed orders increased considerably and once again the industry began to flourish. Markets were established in mainland Australia, New Zealand, Europe, USA and the Canary Islands. In the early 1970s, Alan Williams (husband of Lena Thompson), was appointed the Board's agent.

Concerned that Lord Howe Island was no longer the only source of fertile seeds, Alan visited European buyers in 1976, to learn how they were propagating the seeds. Upon his return, the Board supported his proposal of a trial propagation program on the Island. The trial was successful and in 1977 the first seedlings were exported, with enormous response from existing seed buyers and new markets. Nurseries still wanted descendants of the 'mother stock' growing in their natural environment.

Following the success of this program, the Board's Palm Nursery was established in 1978. The demand for Kentia palm seedlings increased rapidly and by 1981 the export of seeds had ceased.

As its enterprise grew, the Board sought professional assistance from the New South Wales Department of Agriculture. Consequently in 1985, Chris Weale was seconded to manage the Nursery. Under his guidance, markets were expanded and quality control became a priority. With further assistance from the Department of Agriculture, the Nursery achieved ISO 9001:2000 quality accreditation in 1995.

Chris also instigated the training of Islanders in horticulture. Larry Wilson is now the Nursery Manager overseeing a staff of six permanent employees and several casual workers. The Nursery turns over approximately $1m per year, of which the revenue flows back into the administration of the Island. Of the 1.5 to 2 million seedlings sold per year, 90% are exported to Henk van Staalduinen and his son Rob, owners of a major nursery in Holland. They have been buying the Island's palm seedlings for twenty-eight years, and have formed a close relationship with the Island and its people.

Although the Nursery's income is derived mainly from its trade in Kentia palm seedlings, it also exports Curly palm seedlings as well as seeds and seedlings of Big and Little Mountain palms. In recent years it has also been responsible for the propagation of other endemic plants for revegetation on the Island.

During the 1980s, Islanders once again sought a direct stake in the palm seed industry. While the Board was establishing its own Nursery, a palmgrowers' cooperative comprising twelve families was formed in conjunction with Sydney nurseryman Gary Andreasen. Representations were made to the Board, which agreed to sell an annual quota to the cooperative. Although the cottage based industry flourished for a time, politics and relocation of some members to the mainland saw the cooperative defunct by the late 1990s. However, in 2004 an amendment to the Lord Howe Island Act allowed Perpetual leaseholders ownership of palms on their leases; and a financial interest in their cultivation.

ADMINISTRATORS AND THE BOARD

Government House, circa 1910

'Uncle Willie' Thompson

Courtesy of LHI Historical Society

Although control of Lord Howe Island was initially vested in the British Crown, and later in the New South Wales Parliament, the early settlers were too distant and too small in number to warrant much attention from the authorities. The only consideration given to the Island between 1835 and 1869, was when the Government sought a suitable place to offload the worst offenders of its convict stock.

After Surveyor Fitzgerald's visits in 1869 and 1876, he advised the Colonial Secretary that the Islanders lived in a relatively harmonious and self-regulating community. However, recognition of the unique flora and fauna during his visits prompted a keener interest, and in 1878 the Government proclaimed the Island a Forest Reserve. Later that year, Captain Armstrong was appointed the first Administrator.

When Armstrong was removed from office in 1882 four magistrates of varying calibre, Messrs Wilkinson, Icely, Brodie and Farnell, administered the Island until 1913. They visited on an annual basis unless urgent matters required their presence more often. Brodies Point, near Middle Beach and Farnell Park, which is today the cricket/sports ground, were named after two of these Magistrates.

Frank Farnell did more to benefit the Island than his predecessors. He succeeded in obtaining Government grants to build a jetty, construct roads, re-open the schoolhouse and clear recreation grounds. He also formed the Kentia Palm Seed Cooperative on behalf of the Islanders. Farnell retired in 1910.

As a result of two Royal Commissions in 1911 and 1912 a Lord Howe Island Board of Control, comprising three members, was appointed in 1913. The Chairman was the Under-Secretary of the Chief Secretary's Department, and two members represented the Department of Agriculture. The Board carried out its deliberations in Sydney, with decisions being conveyed to the Island residents by circulars sent on a quarterly basis. Once a year, as the Magistrates had done before them, the Board members visited the Island and made courtesy calls on residents to solicit their views on local issues of the day.

Under the watchful but distant eye of the mainland Board, a three-man Local Advisory Committee was formed to carry out policy decisions adopted by the Board. All positions were of an honorary capacity. The Committee Chairman was a permanent appointee; the position held by W S Thompson until his death in 1953, at the age of 85. Two Islanders were elected by their peers on a biennial basis.

A delicate balance between mainland and Island interests continued until 1940, when World War II severely affected the Island's palm seed trade and tourist industry. Subsequently the Board appointed an agricultural expert, Mr C Ahrens, as resident Superintendent to oversee a farming program that would encourage the Islanders to become self-sufficient, and assist in the war effort. However, this administrative posting was not welcomed by the residents who, prior to that appointment, had begun supplying mainland establishments with fruit, vegetable and flower seeds. By 1940 their gardens were producing acres of tomatoes and, as Sydney seed merchants Yates and Rumseys proclaimed – seeds of the world's finest rockmelon, watermelon and cucumbers. Mr Ahrens remained only a short time and was replaced by Mr Kennett.

After the War, requests by Islanders to have the office of resident Superintendent made redundant were ignored, which prompted Gerald Kirby to comment: -

> The only three bodies of people ruled by Superintendents are the Aborigines, the Insane and the Lord Howe Islanders.

The office was retained and the Superintendent's duties were increased to administrate on most of the Island's affairs. Consequently the Local Committee lost much of its influence and continued to function only in a limited capacity as advisor to the Board.

Since 1879 administration had been based on Government proclamations. However, primarily because of issues relating to land tenure, a specific parliamentary bill was introduced in 1953; making Lord Howe Island the only place in New South Wales to be governed by its own Act of Parliament. The preamble to this Act began under "Act No 39, Lord Howe Island", which stated:

> An Act to make provision for the care, control and management of Lord Howe Island; to constitute a Lord Howe Island Board and an Island Committee and to define their prospective powers, authorities, duties and function; to make provision relating to the tenure of land upon the said Island; to validate certain matters; and for purposes connected therewith.

With the passing of the Act, the Board of Control was reconstituted as the Lord Howe Island Board and comprised five members instead of three. For the first time, Islanders were allowed to elect one representative to the Board. Of the four other members, the Chairman remained the Under-Secretary of the Chief Secretary's Department (until governance was transferred to other departments), one was the local member of State Parliament and two were Ministerial appointees. The Advisory Committee was retained and was made up of four elected Islanders.

Over the next two decades, major changes and outside influences affected Island politics and, by the late 1970s, the Act in its present form was considered outdated. In 1981 an Amendment Act abolished the Island Committee; and Islanders were given three elected positions (including that of Vice-Chairman) on a new five-man Board. The Chairman remained a representative of the governing department, and an officer was appointed by the Minister responsible for the National Parks & Wildlife Service Act, 1974. Board meetings, once held in Sydney, were replaced by public meetings on the Island on a quarterly basis with some deliberations being conducted in camera.

Although it was the first time Islanders held a majority of seats on their own local government authority, it came with a price. Allegations of conflicts of interest specifically in land, and later on in shipping matters, led to a Public Accounts enquiry in 1990, followed by two investigations by the Independent Commission against Corruption (ICAC). While no evidence of corrupt practice was found ICAC's report *Preserving Paradise, good governance guidance for small communities – Lord Howe Island,* and a National Competition Policy review of the Act, resulted in Parliament passing an Amendment Bill in 2004.

Under the new provisions, Board membership increased to seven – three appointed members and four elected Islanders. While the latter retain a majority, their voting power is still often limited by perceived conflicts of interest. In this small isolated community where most families are related, and major issues confronting the Board affect everyone, many feel the criteria pertaining to conflicts of interest should be relaxed. If unable to cast a vote on a particular issue a member's input into its discussion is, at the very least, considered important by the 200 or more voters who seek fair representation on the Board.

The Board is responsible for all local government functions. From humble beginnings in a small office in Government House, to its present office complex nearby, today it employs about twenty-four permanent staff and several casual workers. Included in its duties are electricity generation, aerodrome management, waste management, weed control, maintenance of public roads, buildings and recreational facilities, and supervision of the Island's tourist and palm industry. It also conducts the only licenced liquor distribution outlet, but is empowered to grant permits to other commercial establishments for the sale of alcohol.

The original liquor store was established at the Public Hall in 1955. The first supplies arrived on the *Sorona del Mar* on 12 October and trading commenced a week later for one hour on Mondays, Wednesdays and Fridays.

Various mainland government departments have controlled the administration of Lord Howe Island for 93 years – from the Chief Secretary's Department in 1913, Lands Department in 1955, Premier's Department in 1983, Local Government in 1986 and the National Parks & Wildlife Service since 1988. During this time it was also shunted from one electorate to another. Currently it remains in the Port Macquarie electorate from where the servicing of police and distance education are provided.

There have been twenty-two administrators since 1939. Four Islanders have temporarily held the position between mainland appointments. Of the other administrators – one was forcibly removed, another died in office, one served two terms and four were short-term appointments of six months. Horton Ward, the longest serving superintendent, held the position for sixteen years. Judy Mortlock, the only female administrator, served nine years. The remaining nine appointments were for periods of two to five years. Government House accommodated the mainland administrators.

Built in 1890 as a residence for the visiting magistrates, Government House has also played host to two NSW Governors – Sir Dudley de Chair in 1927 and Sir Phillip and Lady Game in 1933. For some years after their marriage, Edith and George Kirby lived in a small cottage on the property as caretakers.

Between official visits, and before its occupation by resident administrators, Government House served another purpose. As a venue for the Island's young bloods in many a romantic tryst, the visits, although not official were probably a lot more fun! Bookings were essential and, in the absence of a reception office, an over-sized vegetable identifying the amorous rake would be placed by the door – reserving the house for the evening.

17

LAND TENURE AND WORLD HERITAGE

The story of land tenure on Lord Howe Island is a tale of monumental frustration for generations of families whose forebears began as squatters in Paradise. The fight for security over title of their land spanned 106 years.

It began in 1847 when Captain Poole and Dr. Foulis abandoned the settlement, after the Government rejected their application for freehold title over the lands they occupied. The Andrews, Moselys, Wrights and Middletons remained although the latter two families would later leave. The Thompson family and other settlers soon arrived and by the mid 1850s, Lord Howe Island was a small but thriving community. A variety of local produce was traded with whalers and exported to the mainland market. With their livelihood dependent on the land, it was only natural for these farmers to seek secure title over their land.

When Commander Challis visited the Island on HMS *Rosario* in 1871, the residents asked him to submit to the State Governor their need to have a long lease or absolute gift of the land they were cultivating. He passed their request on to his superiors in Sydney, but the matter ended there.

After the Government granted Captain Armstrong a 100-acre lease in 1878, the Islanders again sought security over their tenure. This led to the first official survey of lands for cultivation on the Island; upon which a small number of short-term leases (Permissive occupancies) were then granted to Islanders. However, the legality of these leases was in doubt as the provisions of the Crown Lands Act 1875, under which the leases were granted, failed to mention Lord Howe Island. Prior to that the Island merited only a brief mention in the Constitution Act 1856, which transferred legislative power from Britain to the New South Wales State Parliament. It was completely ignored again in the Crown Lands Consolidation Act 1884, in which the Eastern Division of the State was defined as the waters of the Pacific Ocean.

In his 1882 report to the Government after the Armstrong Inquiry, John Bowie Wilson included the following recommendation on Island land tenure: -

> no more persons be allowed to settle on the Island other than existing residents and their families, who should be granted leases for a ten year period

John Bowie Wilson's recommendation was also ignored.

The first of the visiting Magistrates, Henry Wilkinson, begged the Government to give consideration to Islanders' rights for a reasonable security of tenure; and the allocation of sufficient land for their requirements. This led to a Code of Regulations for the Island in 1883. These bylaws embodied the recommendations put forward by Magistrate Wilkinson and received the approval of the Islanders. However, before the Code could receive Executive Council sanction, the Government of the day retired from office and the matter was forgotten.

Magistrate Brodie pleaded the Islanders' case in 1898. This prompted yet another survey that recommended the inclusion of Lord Howe Island as part of a Land District in New South Wales. This was not put into effect as it would have required an amendment to the existing Crown Lands Act.

Magistrate Farnell took up the Islanders' grievances in 1905, after thirteen residents petitioned him to obtain Government approval to convert their Permissive occupancies to Freehold title. Frank Farnell, who had been granted a Permissive occupancy in 1903, strongly supported their case. However, any changes to land tenure would also have required amendments to existing legislation. Consequently the matter was shelved yet again.

Seven years later there was a glimmer of hope! Because of the difficulties arising in the Kentia Palm Seed industry, the State Government appointed two Royal Commissions of Inquiry into the trade, and the welfare of the Islanders. Walter Bevan, who led the second Commission in 1912, was instructed to find some equitable system of land tenure that would secure effective and stable settlement of the present residents of the Island and their descendants. His report recommended the constitution of a Board of Control to manage the affairs of Lord Howe Island on behalf of the Government. He further recommended that the proposed Board be empowered to grant:

   a) special homestead leases up to 21 years of about 5 acres

   b) grazing leases to the respective occupants over the balance of
        the land now held by them, for short periods

The Lord Howe Island Board of Control was duly appointed in 1913. All existing Permissive occupancies were revoked; and the Board was granted a Permissive occupancy over all the land on the Island. However, it ignored Walter Bevan's recommendations on land tenure for the Islanders, who were now no more than the tenants of a feudal landlord.

Another 40 years would pass before the Government was forced to acknowledge, the land rights of Lord Howe Islanders. In that time the following attempts were made to correct the injustice: -

1923:- Surveyor Ferrier recommended that more secure tenure be given to Island residents.

1940:- Board Member, R Hicks, visited the Island and recommended that long term tenure be granted to all Island residents.

1946:- The Hon D Clyne, MLA for King and local parliamentary representative, forwarded a petition to the Government signed by 94 landholders and prospective landholders, requesting secure leaseholds subject to certain conditions.

1948:- Board Chairman, W F Sheahan, visited the Island and recommended that Parliament introduce legislation to provide a system of Perpetual and Special leases for Island residents.

1951:- The Hon Clive Evatt QC, Chief Secretary of New South Wales, in a controversial move, recommended the granting of 99-year leases to Islanders subject to certain conditions. Although it was rumoured that the Board opposed the granting of such leases, some were issued on Mr Evatt's authority. (These leases were withdrawn when the Government adopted the 1948 recommendation to introduce special legislation for the Island.)

This proposal, at a time when some Islanders were agitating for self-government, only created a rift within the community. While it offered a measure of security for the first time the conservative group, who liked the way things were and did not want independence from the Board, believed that the leases could be too easily sold to mainland interests. At a meeting on the Island in December 1950, before the recommendation was put to Parliament, their request for Mr Evatt to remove the clause permitting conditional transfer of leases outside the Island caused many heated arguments.

Local Advisory Committee member Roy Wilson, son of Gower and Ada Wilson, said at the time: -

> Who runs this Island, Mr Evatt or the Board of Control? There has been trouble and quarrelling ever since he (Evatt) set foot. He scarcely seemed to listen when we placed before him our views on land tenure. Mr. Evatt practically turned his back on Committee Chairman, W. Thompson, and in my opinion treated him outrageously. Thompson is over 80 years of age and that alone merits courtesy. I heard later that Evatt referred to me as a 'boneheaded adolescent' and he told Tom Payten, third member of the Committee, that he could order him off his land at 5 minutes notice.

William Thompson, Tom Payten and Roy Wilson were Island-born and bred, and occupied land once held by their fathers. William had served as Chairman of the Local

Advisory Committee for 40 years. Tom was 45 years old and within six months of the meeting with Mr Evatt he would lose his life at sea. Roy, the *boneheaded adolescent*, was 26 years old and had served in World War II. He was also the recipient of a George Cross for bravery, after rescuing two men from the tail-section of a blazing Catalina that had crashed on Malabar in 1948, killing seven of its crew. Roy and his brother Allen owned Ocean View guest house which their father had established more than 40 years before.

The leader of the anti-Board faction was Gerald Kirby, son of Edith and George, and part-owner of Pinetrees. He issued circulars criticising the Board to Island residents and Members of Parliament. The 2500 word documents contained instances of the arbitrary and therefore possibly illegal actions taken by the Board since 1913. To make his point, Gerald included the Board's attempt to have his vehicle licence cancelled and its halving of the Island's beer supply in 1936, which he said *was a crime in Australia ranking just below treason!*

After the release of the circulars, and further agitation within the corridors of power, Gerald and a number of other Island residents engaged the eminent constitutional lawyer, Garfield Barwick QC (later knighted), to advise them on their land rights. In Barwick's opinion, there was no authority in the Executive Council to create the Board of Control in 1913; or to give it any of the powers it possessed. On a visit to the Island, at which he addressed a number of meetings, he stated: -

> The right and power of the Crown, whether by itself or by its delegate in New South Wales, to deal with land was, and in my opinion still is, governed by the Statutes of England affecting the disposal of Crown land. English Common Law stipulates that any person who resides on a piece of land for 60 years or longer automatically becomes its owner, entitled to Freehold title or its equivalent

Unfortunately, the Islanders were not wealthy enough to test Garfield Barwick's opinion in the High Court. Meanwhile, the State Government introduced special legislation and the Lord Howe Island Act, with its restrictive leasehold land tenure cramped by a multitude of stringent conditions, was swept through Parliament in 1953. Sir Henry Manning, MP condemned the Government saying: -

> This appeals to me as being one of the most outrageous exhibitions of expropriation that this Parliament has ever dealt with.

Security of tenure may have been achieved but, after more than a century of continuous occupation of their land, many Island families felt cheated of freehold title.

Under the Act, all land remained the property of the Crown. Direct descendants of Islanders who held Permissive occupancies in 1913 were granted Perpetual leases on blocks of up to 5 acres (2.023 ha) for residential purposes. Short-term Special leases on larger tracts were also granted for pastoral and agricultural activities. Surveyor Mulley carried out a survey for the leases in 1954. (Mulley Drive was named after that surveyor.)

Fifty-one Perpetual leases and forty-three Special leases were notified in the Government Gazette on 18 February 1955. However, the tale was far from over. The conditions attached to Perpetual leases were similar to those laid out by Clive Evatt when he recommended the granting of 99-year leases, and included: -

- a person could not hold more than one lease

- the Island had to be the leaseholders' permanent place of residence

- a lease could transfer by will only to the lineal descendant of an Islander

- a lease was transferable by sale to outside interests provided no Islander expressed an interest

Several properties exchanged hands during the 1960s and 1970s. The sale price was determined by a valuer through the Board. Unfortunately, there were a few instances of properties being withdrawn from the market when other Islanders expressed an interest. Only after those Islanders had satisfied their requirements elsewhere were the properties then sold to mainlanders for a higher price. These dealings led to feelings of anger and betrayal within the community.

The arrival of outsiders created friction between splinter groups of Islanders and non-Islanders. (The latter good humouredly conferred the acronym 'FUNIC' upon themselves – the meaning of which is deemed unfit for publication!) By the end of the 1970s non-Islanders were agitating for equal rights to Islanders. They felt the Act discriminated against them as they were denied representation on the Island Committee, and future land rights for their children were non-existent. Their grievances, together with a growing concern within the Board and mainland conservation groups for a balance between land tenure, administrative decisions and environmental values, led to Parliament passing the Lord Howe Island Amendment Act in 1981. Under this new Act, political and land rights were extended to include all settlers who had resided on the Island for a period of ten years.

It was hard to accept for many who felt the Act now discriminated against Islanders descended from the first settlers. After all, it had taken more than a century for the Government to recognise *their* families' rights; yet less than three decades to grant the same entitlements to those still classed as 'outsiders'. In addition, a number of Islanders pursuing careers on the mainland, returned home to register their status for fear of it being revoked during a long absence. Under the new law, loss of Islander status meant that upon their return, Islanders would have to fulfill the ten-year residency requirement to reclaim the status they inherited at birth.

The new Act abolished future allotment of large leaseholds and introduced a monetary value on the acquisition of land. Lease rentals were set at $200 per hectare, which could be reviewed only every ten years. Any increase could not exceed $100 per hectare.

Apart from governance issues; in order to maintain an adequate revenue base for the Island's management and services, the Act was again amended in 2004. This Bill removed the rent setting provision, enabling the Board to make regulations to set annual rentals. Under this provision, the new time frame for determining rentals was reduced to a minimum of three years, and takes into account advice from the Valuer-General as well as the budgetary circumstances of the Board.

In 2005 land tenure and the eligibility to acquire land remains a contentious issue. In particular is the transfer of property by will which, under the provisions of the Act, a transferee must be the lineal descendant of an Islander. However, on occasions even they have been denied their inheritance. Since 1947, six years before the 1953 Act was passed, five lease transfers by will have caused controversy: -

1947: George Nichols, unable to bequeath his property to his son Mick who held his own lease, willed it to his grandson Barney. The transfer was blocked because Barney was a minor at the time of George's death. The Board of Control purchased the property from the estate for a teacher's residence.

1955: Lil Nichols willed her property to Roy Wilson. At the time of her death, Roy also held another lease and could not take the transfer. (This provision in the Act was later amended.) The house was sold to another Islander.

1982: Jean Brearley, a widow with no children, left her property to David Moxon. David was a former principal of the local school who retained a close relationship with Jean and the Islanders after his term expired. As a non-Islander he was forced to sell the property, which was purchased by an Islander.

1991: Ruby Thompson willed her property, which included a Special lease, to her nephew Lance Wilson. At the time of her death Lance was still employed on the mainland and, although a born Islander, he was unable to meet the residency requirement to retain it. He sold the Perpetual lease to residents who had gained Islander status under the Amendment Act. Although Lance had previously relinquished part of his Special lease, he wished to keep a portion for a future building block. However, the Board resumed the lease on the grounds that under the Act, only the holder of a Perpetual lease was entitled to a Special lease. Lance successfully contested this in the Supreme Court, and today is happily ensconced on a piece of the land that was his inheritance.

2003: Jim Dorman, an Islander under the Amendment Act, was a bachelor and died without issue. He left his estate to mainland relatives, and a sister on the Island with properties of her own. By mutual agreement Jim's niece, Gina Waters, became the sole owner of the house. However, Gina was neither the lineal descendant of an Islander, nor had she gained Islander status. Consequently, after a residency of two years, she was forced to put the property on the market.

In its efforts to resolve the matter satisfactorily, the Board advised Gina to apply to the Minister for the Environment to grant her Islander status in order to retain the property. Her application was denied. As an option, the Board suggested Gina rent the house from the estate until she fulfilled the residency requirement – in another eight years! This is not an option for Gina who still has an obligation to the other beneficiaries.

The intent of the Lord Howe Island Act, 1953 was to ensure properties remained in Islander ownership. While Islanders still have first option to buy, the provision that allows the sale of a property to an outsider appears contradictory when a buyer, at the time of purchase, does not require Islander status. Yet, the beneficiary of a will, including a lineal descendant, must have or be in a position to meet that requirement in order to retain a property. There are currently a dozen or more leaseholders who will face this dilemma in the future.

The issue is compounded by the fact that the Island has nearly reached the number of properties and population it can sustain; and there are more residents wanting land than there are sites available. However, the 2005 Amendments to the Regional Environmental Plan have allowed for the allocation, by ballot, of another twenty-five leases over a period of twenty years. These blocks will be created from current Perpetual leaseholds whose owners have sufficient land, and are willing to subdivide; and from five of the seventeen Special leases still held by Island families since 1953, which have been resumed by the Board for residential purposes. The revoking of these leases, and allotment by ballot, has naturally angered those leaseholders, their children and other descendants of the first settlers who, under this system, could very well miss out on obtaining their own piece of land. As one Islander succinctly put it – *the Government is literally raffling off our heritage!*

There are approximately 122 leases on Lord Howe Island today. Of this number 83 are occupied by lineal descendants, and 25 by other Islanders and residents of less than ten years. Another 14 homes are occupied by Government employees.

Because of its many outstanding characteristics, Lord Howe Island and its adjacent islets were inscribed on the World Heritage List on 14 December 1982, under the UNESCO Convention concerning the protection of world cultural and national heritage. At that time there was an approximate total of 83 leaseholds. The 1981 Amendment Act proclaimed a Permanent Park Preserve over the untouched nature reserves at the north and south ends of the Island. Supervision of the Preserve was recommended under a Plan of Management code prepared by the NSW National Parks & Wildlife Service. To control development in the settled central area of the Island, the Amendment Act brought the Board within the provisions of the NSW Environmental Planning and Assessment Act 1979, which required a Regional Environmental Plan as a guide for future growth. A Regional Environmental Study was completed in 1985; and the Regional Environmental Plan (REP) for the Island was gazetted in 1986. Since then the REP, its current amendments, and proposed changes to the Permanent Park Preserve that would allow areas for eco-tourism campers, have caused considerable controversy.

A balance for land tenure and environmental values on this small Heritage site has attracted much outside attention. An Island majority on the Board is regarded by some mainland groups as disproportionate to the relatively small but privileged community it serves; and should not be allowed to dominate the decision making which affects long-term function of the Island, the amenity it provides for visitors, and the image cherished by the rest of the world. Understandably, there is a great sense of frustration when Islanders hear these groups express such opinions on issues that affect *their* lives and future. Lord Howe Island was not listed on cultural grounds; and theorists on World Heritage values forget that, long before 1982, Islanders in earning that 'privileged' status, had developed a distinctive social structure and a unique identity, which many feel is now in danger of disappearing.

18

IMPACT OF PREDATORS

The sporadic but heavy predation on Lord Howe Island's bird life by mariners and early settlers, which resulted in the extinction of two species of landbirds and one species of seabird, was compounded by the introduction of feral animals.

Goats and pigs were introduced in the early 1800s as a food source for whalers. However, they made a huge impact on the Island's avifauna. Goats destroyed or reduced the low shrubs and grasses that formed the protected nesting areas of many land and seabirds. Pigs ate the eggs and young chicks of both species. Also, in their hunt for edible plant roots, tubers, earthworms and other food, their foraging habits disturbed large areas of leaf-litter and ground-cover, depleting the food chain for a number of landbirds.

Seabirds were driven from their nesting grounds in the northern hills, shoreline slopes, headlands and lowland sand dunes, to the safety of the summit of the southern mountains or offshore islets.

In the 1840s black cats were released from a provisioning whaleship and quickly multiplied. They found easy prey among the pigeons, parrots and woodhens, decimating the former two and driving the latter to the summit of Mount Gower and the upper slopes of Mount Lidgbird.

As the birdlife decreased, the number of injurious insects increased. Caterpillars, fruit flies (not the species to inhabit the Island in the 1950s) and centipedes destroyed the produce of Island gardens. The coccus insect also inflicted a great deal of damage to the banyan trees.

Mice were accidentally introduced from Norfolk Island in 1860. Despite being defined as a rodent that commensally lives with humans, their only contribution to the Island was to annihilate the destructive centipede.

The greatest tragedy to Lord Howe Island's avifauna was the arrival of black rats in June 1918. After striking an unmarked rock in the Admiralty Group, the Burns Philp steamer *Makambo* was run aground on Neds Beach. Cargo was removed while repairs were effected and, although there were no eyewitness accounts, it is believed the rats escaped from the offloaded cargo and bilge of the vessel into the Island forests.

Within a year these predators, by then numbering in the thousands, wreaked havoc through the Island. Another five endemic bird species were decimated – the Lord Howe Island Starling, Fantail, Fly-eater, Vinous-tinted Blackbird (Doctor bird) and the Robust White-eye.

The rats also took their toll on the Island's endemic invertebrates including the land snail and giant phasmid, locally known as the land lobster. (The phasmid was thought to be extinct until 2001, when Island rangers discovered a small colony living on Balls Pyramid.)

In the 1920s the Island's economy depended largely on the palm seed industry. The rats, having preyed on the insectivorous birds that helped control damage to seeds by destructive weevils, then attacked the palm seeds.

The Board of Control's initial attempts to eradicate the rats with Barium chloride poison proved unsuccessful. The poison was dispersed openly in the bush and not placed in proper feeding stations. Unfortunately, it too took a heavy toll on the remaining birdlife.

It was then made mandatory for all shareholders in the palm seed industry to devote one day per fortnight to the hunting of rats. The Board supplied them with traps, shotguns and ammunition. A series of bounties were placed on the rats, with the severed tails being proof of their destruction. Payment of 1d per tail in 1920, gradually increased to 6d in 1928. The extent to which rats had overrun the Island was evidenced by the number of tails delivered for payment – 13,771 in 1927, and 21,214 in 1928. Later the bounty decreased as new control measures came into force.

An Island anecdote relates how a churchgoer gave a rat's tail in the church collection plate. However, when the income of the bounty hunters increased with a hefty payment of 2/6d per tail for pigs, the same churchgoer offered a pig's tail and took change out in coinage!

After World War II, poison baits were introduced but 'ratting' continued into the 1950s as a new generation of Islanders sought pocket money of 3d per tail. By then the Board realised that total eradication was impossible. However, ratting was a method that brought a measure of control while providing a remunerative sideline for the Islanders.

Between 1922 and 1930, in a further effort to combat the rats, the Board imported 80 Masked Owls from the Taronga Zoological Park Trust and several overseas areas, including the San Diego Zoo in California. This scheme was also ineffective. It was as though the owls formed a pact with the rats to share predatory rights on many of the birds! This prompted the Island verse: -

Owls were imported to eat the rats that ate the birds that ate the weevils that ate the seeds that grew on the palms of Lord Howe Island

Ironically, the introduction of Masked Owls probably caused the extinction of the Lord Howe Island Boobook – an owl endemic to the Island. While the rats did not directly threaten the Boobook, it probably suffered too much competition from the introduced owls which were larger and stronger. The Masked Owls commandeered the better nesting sites, and were more successful in the hunt for food. The Boobook was last seen on the Island in the 1950s.

Today the Lord Howe Island Board uses the Warfarin based poison Ratsak to control the rats. It is dispensed from specially made feeding stations comprising a T-shaped assembly of white PVC plumber's pipe. These stations are constructed to exclude all animals excepts rats and mice.

Household pets also played their role in the war against predators, until they too were considered a threat to the Island's avifauna. Dogs (mostly fox terriers) were used to hunt rats and pigs, and domestic cats made a huge impact on the mice population. When a Parliamentary ban on the importation of cats was introduced, under the 1981 Amendments to the Lord Howe Island Act, it was met with mixed emotions from the Islanders. However, after a ministerial ban on dogs was imposed in 1989, Islanders were justifiably enraged when a newly appointed public servant was permitted to import a dog. Subsequently, the dog ban was lifted in 1996. Today, the number of dogs on the Island probably exceeds the dog population before the ban. Although the Parliamentary ban on cats remains in place, one lonesome puss still exists. Indeed, after twenty-four years, 'Tasman' gives credence to the old adage that a cat has nine lives!

When programs were introduced to eradicate feral animals in the late 1970s, the goats were decimated from the northern hills, and their numbers culled considerably in other areas. Although seabirds began to recolonise former habitats in the hills, they did not return to the lowland areas they once occupied. The Fleshy-footed shearwater, or muttonbird, is the only seabird that inhabits a large portion of the settlement area today.

In recent years, areas have been determined as important breeding grounds for several seabirds including the Sooty tern (wideawake), Red-tailed tropic bird (bosun bird), Masked booby, Black-winged petrel, Noddy and Wedge-tailed shearwater. These areas are constantly monitored to guard against human impact.

The feral pig and cat populations were also successfully eradicated, and landbirds began to recolonise.

The woodhen, one of the few endemic species to survive all predatory impacts, was still an endangered species and by the late 1970s, it was estimated that only 37 remained. Between 1980 and 1984, the National Parks & Wildlife Foundation sponsored a woodhen captive-breeding project in Stevens Reserve. With assistance from the Board the program was a resounding success. No longer confined to refuges in the mountains, woodhens now roam freely through the lowlands and are classed as pets around many Island homes.

Lord Howe Island's bird life may never again be compared to Ovid's Golden Age, as it was by Arthur Bowes in 1788. However, today as a haven for original species, and new species through the natural process of migration, the Island still reflects an image of a distant time. And the woodhen surely has to be the timekeeper.

Courtesy of Ian Hutton

Lord Howe Island Woodhen

19

THE WAR AGAINST WEEDS

Friends of Lord Howe Island

Undesirables of another kind have also impacted on the environment. The year 2005 marked the tenth anniversary of the first volunteer weeding trip to Lord Howe Island. In March 1995, concern over the expanding noxious weed problem prompted Ian Hutton to approach the Board Manager, Judy Mortlock, with a proposal to bring nine weeders from Canberra and Sydney. A program was approved and the group arrived the following June. Mornings were dedicated to removing infestations of Ground asparagus from Transit Hill, while the afternoons were given to exploring the Island's environment. The week-long visit was such a success it set the scene for future tours.

In 1996 and 1997, Ian organised six trips for Australian Academic Tours, in which participants were given optional half days weeding. Most group members did volunteer, and over 250 hours were spent in removing dense areas of Ground asparagus. In 1998 another visit was run by Sydney bush generator Rymill Abell, similar to Ian's programs. Twenty-nine people were involved in this tour, which was repeated in 1999. The enthusiasm shown by the weeders instigated the formation of the Friends of Lord Howe Island group in 2000. The visitations subsequently grew to six each winter; and pioneered treatment methods to eradicate both Ground and Climbing asparagus. Vast sections of the Island's settlement area and Transit Hill have since been cleared of these weeds. In 2002, each group provided one morning of labour to assist the Board with removal of Bridal creeper from the Middle Beach cliff area.

To encourage Island residents to weed their leases, the volunteer groups have assisted in treating both asparagus species, Cherry guava, Ochna, Cotoneaster, Madeira vine and Cestrum on several private properties. They have also been involved in planting native trees at Middle Beach, Old Settlement and Cobbys Corner.

Since these eradication programs began, there have been thirty trips and over 10,000 hours of voluntary labour given to weed removal. These visitors are indeed friends of Lord Howe Island.

Friends in action

123

20

THE TOURIST INDUSTRY

The climate of the Island is most equable, and the scenery beautiful. An increasing number of visitors can be expected (Walter Bevan, Royal Commission, 1912)

When Burns Philp & Company established a steamer trade between Sydney, Lord Howe Island and Norfolk Island in 1893, it began a passenger service to the latter port to supplement the cargo carrying trade. En route they were occasionally offered 24-hour respite at Lord Howe when adverse sea conditions delayed the discharge of cargo. The Islanders enjoyed the social contact with the passers-by who, in turn, were captivated by the Island's natural charm and the hospitality of its residents. These short sojourns prompted Burns Philp to quietly promote Lord Howe as a holiday destination.

To cater for longer-term visitors was a gamble. It required improvements on land which, without title, could be resumed by the Government without notice. Nevertheless, by 1900 Mary Nichols had added extra rooms to the family homestead, renamed it The Pines, and was operating the first guest house on Lord Howe Island.

The Pines, circa 1900

Steamer Day

After a two day voyage from Sydney, passengers were landed by sling into open boats manned by crews of three rowers plus one to steer. Close to shore, the oarsmen went overboard and carried the passengers to the beach, first the men on their backs and then the women in their arms. From the beach the visitors either walked or rode on horse-drawn sleighs to the The Pines. There they enjoyed nine days bushwalking, swimming, fishing and beachcombing, followed by musical evenings at the homes of Mary Nichols' children, before embarking on the steamer when it returned from Norfolk.

These excursions became known as the 'short trip' after Burns Philp extended the shipping route to include the New Hebrides (Vanuatu) which, referred to as the 'long trip', afforded visitors a nineteen day stay on the Island.

The duration of these visits periodically increased by multiples of weeks as landing passengers depended on favourable conditions. On a steamer's approach, the Islanders would hoist a flag to signal on which side of the Island it should anchor. A white flag flown from Signal Point meant safe anchorage on the western side; a red flag raised at Jims Point indicated moorage off Neds Beach; and if both flags were flying, neither side was safe. In the event of 'double flags' the steamer lay off the Island until one was lowered or, if weather conditions were extreme, it continued on to the next port. If the latter occurred en route from Sydney, Lord Howe bound passengers if they chose to, could disembark on the return voyage and be picked up on the next trip. After enduring the extra time at sea, most were happy to do so. If anchorage was not possible sailing from Norfolk, visitors due to embark at the Island had no choice but to wait for the next boat. From all accounts these minor disruptions caused little concern. Many years later, a regular visitor was reported as saying: -

> Thank the Lord the Island is three days out on a rough sea. If it weren't, the trippers would have pulled it apart long ago.

With accommodation for ten The Pines offered the only guest lodgings on the Island; until 1909 when Gower and Ada Wilson opened their home to visitors. By 1913, Ocean View was an established guest house catering for seven. However, a year later World War I disrupted the fledgling industry.

After the death of her mother in 1923, Edith Kirby became proprietor of The Pines. She retired from the physical work of the guest house in 1930, handing over the day-to-day operation to her eldest son Gerald, and his wife. Gerald had completed a college education, married Beth Singleton, and was pursuing a career with the Sydney roofing tile company Wunderlichs when Australia was gripped by the Great Depression. He returned to the Island to assist his mother until the economic situation improved, and he could resume his profession on the mainland. However, he did not

Edith Kirby

return to Sydney, and the newly named Pinetrees became Gerald and Beth's lifelong career.

There was a demand for further accommodation after the *Morinda*, equipped to carry forty passengers, replaced the *Makambo* in 1932 as the Island's main service provider.

By 1933, Pinetrees comprised seven double and two single rooms, plus a block of ten single rooms (five back-to-back) known as Virgin's Alley, and Bachelor or Rum Row. In the summer months, when extra visitors were expected, beds were put on verandahs and large tents pitched on the border of the property facing the cricket ground. The southside of the boatshed was converted into five rooms, which were assigned preferentially to the guests who snored! Pinetrees often catered for 75 guests or more over the Christmas period.

Camping style quarters were not confined to Pinetrees alone. Once clear of Sydney, and against maritime regulations, tents were erected on the after-hatch of the *Morinda* to accommodate extra passengers. On the return voyage, they were disassembled before reaching port. Additional provisions were not included in these clandestine operations, so in smooth sailing there was always a shortage of food. However, on a rough trip there was often an over-supply! Two seasoned voyagers, Marj Scott and Bill Shipway (grandson of a founding member of the Kentia Palm Cooperative), recalled that on these journeys it was recommended that passengers stick to toast and strawberry jam because *it tasted just as good coming up as it did going down*!

Ocean View was extended to include double and single rooms in bungalows known as Do Drop In, Venture In and Astor Flats. The guest house also added the luxury of electricity, having a generator installed on the premises in 1933. When Gower was lost at sea in 1936, management of Ocean View passed to his eldest daughter, Eileen and her husband, Tasman Douglass. Gower's sons, Allen and Roy, took over the business after World War II.

Amenities were basic before the introduction of electricity, gas and refrigeration. Pit toilets were erected in the bush, ice chests ran on kerosene, pressure lamps provided lighting and chip heaters were used for hot water. However, what guests lacked in modern conveniences was far outweighed by the hospitality of their hosts. Daily activities included fishing trips and aquaplaning on the lodge-owned launches *Albatross* and *Venture*. There were reef walks, mountain hikes, picnics, barbecues and tennis parties. The dining rooms were renowned for their tables of home cooking. Vegetables, fruit, milk, cream, butter, poultry, beef and pork were all locally produced. Islanders were invited to mingle with visitors at weekly dance nights hosted alternately by the two guest lodges. On these evenings patrons were entertained by an Island orchestra, while their hosts served a seemingly endless supply of supper, cigarettes, liquor and soft drinks – all on the house!

When the *Makambo* ran aground in 1918, it led to a rat plague that almost destroyed the palm seed trade. As the Kentia Palm Seed Cooperative floundered over the next decade, shareholders eager to find alternative income entered the tourist industry. By the late 1930s the Dignam, Whiting and Austic families were taking guests. Early visitors to two of these homes recounted: -

(The Dignam home – Thornleigh)

> A track winding through thicket grove and woodland took us to our abode, so meticulously tidy inside and out. Narrow asphalted paths curve between palms to a verandah that is shaded by a lofty fig tree with massive leaves. The bungalow rambles delightfully and seems to have as many verandahs as rooms on which the family, in leisure moments, spends time entertaining their guests. At the end of one long verandah, the master of the house, Mr. Dignam, has his office where, besides transacting his business as B P agent and butcher, he sells local photographic views and, as the Island's librarian, he has many up-to-date books. At the back of the house is a dairy, orchard, vegetable garden, butcher shop and store, from which he supplies the Island's liquor.

(The Whiting home – Palmhaven)

> Our host, Mr. Whiting, is a placid, good natured man who is very rarely idle. His wife, Sue, is graceful, pretty, well dressed and an enterprising young woman. One room of her bungalow is a store stocked with an inexhaustible supply of luxuries and necessities – bathing suits, cosmetics, photographic materials, refills for torches, sweets and cool drinks. She develops film, does dressmaking to order and is a hairdresser. In between all this she cooks, keeps this charming property spotless and still finds time for her favourite pastimes – tennis and dancing.

Unfortunately, the Whiting's guest house venture was unprofitable and eventually failed. The fault probably lay with Sue who, as a grand hostess and perfectionist,

Sue Whiting

insisted her guests have the best of everything – from the finest linen, china and glassware, to her highly polished silverware. And if the food she prepared for her guests was not to her liking, it was fed to the chooks and she would begin again.

The industry temporarily ceased again during World War II. As shipping became more irregular, sailing schedules were no longer advertised and, by the time the Japanese entered the war in 1941, most of Burns Philp's ships had been mobilised for the war effort. Consequently the passenger service was confined to Islanders travelling to Sydney, where they could then wait up to several months before 'catching the boat home'. The war years marked the end of steamship travel to the Island.

It was during this time that RAAF Catalinas from Rathmines Flying Boat Base on Lake Macquarie, NSW, periodically flew to the Island for medical evacuations or to deliver urgently needed supplies. These flights raised the possibility of a commercial air service. In a 1940 memorandum to residents, the Board of Control stated:

> It is felt that the establishment of a flying-boat service between Sydney and Lord Howe Island would provide a facility that would contribute immeasurably to make Lord Howe Island one of the leading, if not the premier tourist resort of Australia

Further lobbying by Islanders after the war resulted in Captain P G Taylor making a 3-day visit, in December 1946, to assess the suitability of using converted Sunderlands as commercial passenger carriers. Consequently Trans Oceanic Airways began the first flying boat service to Lord Howe Island in 1947. Qantas followed later that year using Catalinas and Sunderlands. However, the competition on such a small route was unprofitable and Qantas withdrew in 1951. Ansett Airways (later Ansett-ANA) took over Trans Oceanic in 1953 and, upon merging with Barrier Reef Airways, formed Ansett Flying Boat Services. In the next nineteen years, the frequency of flights to the Island increased from one a fortnight to six or seven per week during the busy periods. On occasions there were two flights per day. Each flight carried up to 42 passengers.

Islanders responded to the increase with new guest lodges, small businesses and tea houses such as Do Drop Inn and Mountain Inn. Some lodges later changed ownership and were renamed. Leanda Lei, Somerset, Banyan (Lorhiti) and Valdon (Beachcomber) began operating in the 1950s, followed by Sea Breeze (Capella), Blue Lagoon, Coral Court (Howeana), Polynesia (Pandanaus Restaurant) and Tradewinds in the 1960s. The latter, now a private residence, also operated as a nightclub competing with Ollies Cabaret (Larhonette) and Sarong (Somerset). In later years several restaurants opened, some within private homes – Aggies Steak Bar (Kentia), Milky Way, Coral Court Take-Away, Elsies, Admiralty Bar & Grill, Auntie Sues, Up The Garden Path and Blue Peters. Milky Way still operates and Auntie Sues is now Pandanus Restaurant.

As the 1960s progressed, operation of the flying boats became increasingly uneconomical. All efforts to retain them failed and after exhaustive investigation of alternative aircraft, the much loved seaplanes and their lagoon landing pad gave way to a 900-metre airstrip in 1974. Construction was carried out by the Royal Australian Engineers as contractors to the NSW Department of Public Works. The last flying boat was bid a fond farewell on 10 September and commercial use of the airstrip commenced two days later.

Over the next sixteen years, a succession of commuter airlines maintained services from Sydney, Brisbane, Port Macquarie and Coffs Harbour. And, not since the steamship days, a direct link was established with Norfolk Island. All services operated planes that could carry a maximum of ten passengers until 1989, when the Brisbane-based Norfolk Airlines introduced a 36-seat Dash-8 aircraft with short take-off and landing capabilities. When that company went into liquidation in early 1991, the Norfolk Island link ceased and Eastern Australia and Sunstate Airlines (both now Qantaslink) commenced Dash-8 services from Sydney and Brisbane. Commuter airlines continued to run for a time but the operation of small aircraft was severely affected when, in 1994, a locally operated Aero Commander crashed on a flight from Williamtown to Lord Howe, killing all nine people on board.

Qantaslink now provides up to twenty flights per week during the peak season. Approximately 10,000 visitors pass through Lord Howe Island per year; and with environmental and planning safeguards in place, the maximum number of tourists at any one time is set at 400. Also, with a hint of the by-gone whaling era, the Island has once again become an international attraction.

Today, Arajilla, Milky Way, Waimarie, Mary Challis, Ebbtide, Hideaway, Broken Banyan and Earls Anchorage have increased the number of tourist establishments to seventeen. While most are now self-contained apartments, guests have access to several well stocked stores, take-away food facilities and a variety of restaurants and cafes. And, as the only all-inclusive lodge, Pinetrees still provides the service started by Mary Nichols in 1900.

A wide range of activities treat visitors to the Island's history, unique flora and fauna and the aquatic life surrounding the southernmost coral reef in the world.

Since tourism began, the Island has been renowned for its 'return' visitors, referred to as 'the regulars'. Many such as the Bradshaws, Farr-Jones', Rowes and Creers witnessed the growth of the industry from steamship travel in the 1930s, through the flying boat days, and some even to the present era. Third and fourth generations from those early visitors frequent the Island today, and enjoy a friendship with the Islanders as was forged by their forebears. And records have been set! Claude 'Gus' Fay is remembered for his annual month-long visits spanning 30 years; many of which he was accompanied by at least 20 members of his family. Credit for the most number of trips currently belongs to Ron Dingley who, with Peter and Angie Murray close on his heels, has spent sixty-two holidays on Lord Howe – and is still counting! When asked how he managed so many, he quipped: -

Being a bachelor helps!

The industry has also long been a source for matrimony. Since the 1930s, there have been 32 marriages between Islanders and mainlanders employed by the guest lodges. 54 children were born of those unions, followed by 37 grandchildren.

Ocean View, circa 1938

THOSE MAGNIFICENT FLYING MACHINES

Courtesy of LHI Historical Society

Chichester's Madame Elijah (1931), and Pacific Chieftain on take-off

The first plane to land at Lord Howe Island was a Gypsy Moth, a fragile wood and fabric plane fitted with floats and converted into a seaplane. Francis Chichester, on a flight across the Tasman Sea in the *Madame Elijah* in 1931, approached the Island in a severe storm and despite a failed radio, compass and air-speed indicator, he safely landed on the Lagoon. However, as strong winds prevailed during the night, the seaplane capsized on its mooring in Sylphs Hole and was severely damaged. Chichester's fuel stop turned into a 9-week stay while salvage and repairs to his plane were carried out. It was a mammoth task considering the lack of materials, machinery and expertise. Nevertheless, there was plenty of enthusiasm from the Islanders as the men helped rebuild the plane and reassemble the engine, while the women sewed the fabric back on the repaired wings. Chichester chronicled his epic journey in his 1933 book, *Seaplane Solo* (later reprinted as *Alone Over the Tasman*).

As shipping declined during World War II, RAAF Catalinas serviced the Island in the event of emergencies. Further, in 1943 the *Awarua*, an S30 Empire flying boat owned by TEAL, made a forced landing after suffering engine failure while en route from Sydney to Auckland. With the war raging in the Pacific the incident was kept quiet, lest the Island became an enemy target and a strategic point for military operations against mainland Australia. However, the Lagoon's potential prompted post-war lobbying by Islanders for similar aircraft to provide a passenger service. Sunderland and Sandringham flying boats were introduced in 1947.

Although many years would pass before an airstrip was built, several planes landed *on* the Island in the meantime. The first was in October 1947. Harry Newton was flying his small airplane from Europe to New Zealand when he was forced to land on Lagoon Beach. He remained only long enough to have a pee, fix a loose engine cowling with fencing wire, and have rocks removed from the beach to clear a path for take-off. Further landings were made by navy helicopters during an official visit by the Governor-General of Australia, Viscount William D'Lisle in 1962; and by a crop duster in 1968. But, it was the era of the Ansett flying boats that impacted on what has often been described as Lord Howe Island's 'heady' days of tourism.

For many, the experience of travelling on these majestic machines was unforgettable. Providing the last scheduled flying boat service in the world, the planes left Rose Bay in Sydney Harbour to touch down some three hours later on the Island's Lagoon. Flights were timed to arrive at Lord Howe one hour before the high tide, to ensure a maximum depth of water for take-off. As aviation on the Island was restricted to daylight hours, it meant that departures from Rose Bay often occurred in the early hours of the morning. Rather than deter travellers, the wee small hours only added to the romance and excitement of the flying boat adventure. A holiday began the moment the water began lashing against the cabin windows as the aircraft gained momentum and lifted off the harbour into the darkness; leaving the city lights far behind.

The direction for landing was determined by markers placed in the Lagoon from the Department of Civil Aviation's 'crash' boat. Upon reaching its mooring, passengers were ferried by launches from the plane to the jetty where they were greeted by the Ansett agent, David Murray, and their hosts. There they mingled with Islanders and departing visitors. The latter wore leis of hibiscus, frangipani and oleander. Upon leaving the jetty the leis were thrown into the water, hopefully to wash ashore and signify their wearers' return to the Island someday.

Some flights were occasioned by moments of high drama – which only added to the flying boat legend. In one embarrassing incident, passengers were offloaded after a plane suffered minor damage when it began to taxi for take-off while still attached to its mooring! But human error was not always to blame. Being unpressurised aircraft, they could not fly above 10,000 feet and were subject to the vagaries of the weather. On one flight, at an altitude of just 1000 feet, turbulence suddenly lifted the plane another thousand feet, before just as quickly dropping it to 800 feet. Although the aircraft suffered only minor damage to its internal section, the cabin crew sustained serious injuries.

Climatic conditions could change rapidly and therefore dictated flying boat travel. Delays were common, and periodically landings at the Island had to be aborted. There were also layovers of 24 hours or more at Lord Howe when adverse conditions prevented a plane's departure. On three such occasions an aircraft surrendered to the forces of nature. Tragically, the damage inflicted to one flying boat would seal its fate.

Pacific Chieftain, a Sunderland aircraft converted to Sandringham by Shorts at Belfast in 1946, served with Tasman Empire Airlines (later Air New Zealand). She flew under the name RMA *Australia* until she was purchased by Qantas in 1950. As *Pacific Chieftain* she was then bought by Ansett for the Lord Howe Island route in 1954. It was there her service came to an end on 3 July 1963. During a gale she snapped her moorings near Blackburn Island and was beached at Windy Point. She was refloated and taxied to a mooring at Old Settlement but, as conditions worsened, she again broke away and capsized. Irreparably damaged, *Pacific Chieftain* was stripped of all salvageable equipment, taken to sea and committed to the deep.

Beachcomber shared the same beginnings as *Pacific Chieftain*. Flying as RMA *Auckland* until 1950, she was then sold to Barrier Reef Airways and renamed. When Captain Stuart Middlemass merged that company with Ansett, *Beachcomber* began a relationship with Lord Howe Island that would span two decades. While on a layover in June 1974, she too broke her moorings and was beached. Fortunately, Army engineers constructing the airstrip assisted in refloating her, and she was flown back to Sydney. When the flying boat service ceased in September 1974, *Beachcomber* was sold to Captain Charles Blair who, with his actress wife Maureen O'Hara, owned Antilles Air Boats in the Virgin Islands. Under the new name *Southern Cross* she was used for charter work in the Caribbean and, in 1976, provided passenger services between England and Ireland. However after Captain Blair's death in 1977, the aircraft was confined to a hangar in Puerto Rico and fell into decline. In 1980, under the threat of being scrapped, she was taken over by Antilles' chief pilot Ron Gillies, formerly an Ansett flying boat captain. He and other flying boat enthusiasts raised money to have her repaired. The aircraft was then flown to Ireland where she continued charter flights until she was beached at Calshot in 1982. Purchased by the Science Museum, it was eventually decided to house her in the Southampton Hall of Aviation. Transferred there by barge, the aircraft underwent major restoration. Today, she is displayed in the colours that once identified her as Ansett's VH BRC *Beachcomber*.

Islander, an RAF MR.5 Sunderland, was purchased from the New Zealand Air Force in 1963. After conversion to passenger configuration, she replaced *Pacific Chieftain* on the Lord Howe Island run. She narrowly missed the fate of her predecessor when she too washed ashore at Windy Point in May 1965. Islanders and tourists assisted in the massive two week operation to refloat her. She was flown back to Sydney and after undergoing repairs, resumed her run. When the service ended, *Islander* was also sold to Antilles' Air Boats and renamed *Excalibur* VIII. However, US authorities did not recognise Ansett's workshop as an authorised conversion facility, and could not issue a CoA for passenger work. Consequently she was used to provide spare parts for *Beachcomber*. After Captain Blair's death, the aircraft was sold to London businessman, Edward Hulton, and underwent preparation for her flight to Britain in 1981. From there she was flown to Marseilles in France for further restoration work, before being registered for passenger flights in England. However after incurring damage in a gale in 1987, she again underwent extensive repairs. It was at this time that a group of Lord Howe residents, on learning she was for sale, considered the possibility of bringing *Islander* 'home' but the cost involved was prohibitive. In 1993 after auction by Sotheby's failed to reach the reserve price, she was sold privately to an American, Kermit Weekes. Making her last flight in 1996, *Islander* is now housed in her owner's Fantasy of Flight Museum in Florida.

Islander beached at Windy Point (1965)

THE SEA TRADERS

SS Morinda

The Age of Sail may have long passed, but shipping remains a vital trade link between Lord Howe Island and the mainland. When a whaleship appeared on the horizon, the first person sighting it would shout 'Sail-O' at the top of his or her voice. The cry would be picked up by the nearest neighbour who would repeat the call, and so on, until every Islander knew of its impending arrival.

Island Trader

The first regular trader *Rover's Bride* was followed by a succession of similar vessels until 1893, when Burns Philp commenced a steamship service that would include Lord Howe in its Pacific Ocean shipping lanes for the next sixty years. And, two generations of the Dignam family would serve as agents for the Island trade.

As its Pacific island plantations, trading ports and other maritime activities expanded, Burns Philp was often referred to as the 'Hudson Bay Company' of the South Pacific. By the 1930s its fleet consisted of fifteen mainline ships, identified by their black funnels with black and white checkered bands; and countless inter-island sailing and power vessels. The *Morinda* replaced the *Makambo* in 1932 as the main carrier to Lord Howe prior to the war. She was later joined by *Malaita, Muliama* and on occasions *Bulolo*. However, in 1939 trade virtually ceased when most of Burns Philp's ships, their trademark funnels camouflaged, were seconded to the Royal Australian Naval Reserve and Allied Naval Forces for the war effort. Voyages to the Island became few and far between and, with radio blackouts in force, the sighting of a ship was once again signalled by the cry 'Sail-O'.

After the war Burns Philp continued to operate to the Island until 1953, but the service remained irregular with periods of six to twelve weeks between ships. During these long intervals, at the request of the Board of Control, urgent supplies were occasionally brought in by HMAS *Wagga* and other chartered vessels. Also in June 1952, *Malaita* was holed on Neds Beach Reef, incurring a 5-day delay while a diver was flown from Sydney to undertake repairs.

SOMCAL (Societie Maritimes Caledonean) replaced the Burns Philp service to the Island in 1953. Sailing from Noumea via Sydney, the French registered ships *Jacques del Mar, Marie del Mar, Sorona del Mar, Colorado del Mar* and *Damatoag del Mar* operated until the early 1970s. Roy Wilson was appointed the Lord Howe agent. On the evening of 21 July 1954, strong south-westerly winds and rough seas proved fatal for *Jacques del Mar*. While anchored on the western side, she dragged her chain and was washed onto the reef. Her crew was taken to safety during the night but at first light it was obvious that the ship would never leave the reef. Today, what little remains of *Jacques del Mar* off North Bay is a popular site for divers.

The last of the large cargo carrying ships were also French/New Caledonian vessels. *Karlander* (Compagnie des Messageries Maritimes) ran for only a short time. Roy was again appointed agent. *Ile de Lumiere* (Compagnie des Chargeurs) operated from 1972 until 1985, with Clive Wilson (son of Herbert and Lillian) the appointed agent.

In August 1948, a working bee was undertaken at the jetty shed, to add a tea room for the provision of refreshments on 'steamer' days. This service was carried out by members of the Country Womens' Association, and it has often been said that Lil Wilson never missed a day.

The process of unloading freight was time consuming, difficult and often dangerous. Ships anchored offshore either on the western side or off Neds Beach, depending on sea conditions. Cargo was lowered by slings into lighters, which in the early days were rowed ashore and later towed by launches. As Lord Howe was one of several ports serviced on each trip, the time between ships was often six weeks, or longer if the seas delayed despatch of cargo. The commencement of air services had only a small impact as commodities that could be air freighted were limited.

Thus began the quest for smaller vessels capable of entering the Lagoon, berthing at the jetty and servicing Lord Howe Island alone. In the early 1950s, Gerald Kirby purchased the *Flying Cloud*, a 72-foot Fairmile, primarily for tourist trips round the Island and to Balls Pyramid. But Gerald hoped she would also supplement the cargo carrying trade. *Flying Cloud* berthed at the jetty and could carry freight for £14 per ton (compared to £20 on the ships). However, the venture was not successful. The cost of complying with Maritime Services and Union regulations was prohibitive. In addition, she drew too much for the depth of the Lagoon to carry substantial loads. In May 1955 she was beached during a gale and was not refloated for another six months. After Gerald's death in 1960, *Flying Cloud* was sold to mainland interests.

Between 1970 and 1985, a number of small vessels traded for brief periods between Sydney or the North Coast and Lord Howe Island. After about ten trips Gower Wilson's *Trader* was wrecked at Elizabeth Reef while on a fishing expedition. Other boats included *Sol, Barrenjoey, Derwent Hunter* and Norfolk Island's *Norfolk Trader*. The latter two made only two or three trips. The operation of another two trawlers was cut short when they courted disaster in the Lagoon on their first voyage.

In 1985 the mainland owned Lord Howe Island Shipping Company entered with *Kuri Pearl*. Jim Fitzgerald was the appointed agent. During her 9-month service, the Company sent Carl Dignam (son of Phillip jnr and Minnie, nee Fenton) to Europe in search of a more suitable ship for the Island. In September 1986, the 400 tonne Danish coastal trader MV *Sitka* replaced *Kuri Pearl* as the sole operator. However, in 1991 competition emerged with the 487 tonne MV *Island Trader*, one of four sister ships built in Singapore in the early 1980s for coastal trade in New Guinea. Purchased in Cairns by Lord Howe Island Sea Freight, she was the first carrier of bulk fuel to the Island. The Company was formed by residents who believed the Island should have its own ship. Today it is 98% in Island ownership.

Following the introduction of bulk fuel, which was advantageous to the Island aesthetically and economically, two voyages were made by the *Laurana* for the express purpose of removing 7500 unsightly fuel drums from the Island. The drums were shipped to the Solomons for use in the copra industry.

The two ships operated out of Yamba on a fortnightly basis. The trip across took 36 hours, then two days to unload and backload, followed by the return journey. Until they operated on alternate weeks, each trip was a race to secure first use of the Island's jetty. Users of the vessels could be categorized into four groups – those who welcomed a weekly service, die-hard supporters of each ship, and the Board. As a government body, carriage of the Board's goods and fuel, which constitutes over 40% of the Island's cargo, is subject to tender. While both vessels have at times been awarded the contracts, and the tendering process is now outsourced to mainland government departments, the competition has unfortunately been cloaked in controversy. Allegations of corruption, illegal carriage of bulk fuel, oil spills and other environmental damage to the Lagoon, were actively pursued by agitators both on and off the Island. Two inquiries and unwanted media attention in which the competition was referred to as a shipping war, have left many Islanders fearing that one day there will be no shipping service at all.

While competition is desirable in any community, it is hard to sustain in such industries as shipping (and airlines) when the economy is limited by a small population and a ceiling, imposed by law, on tourist numbers. Today, only *Island Trader* services the Island. This could change when the Board's freight contract is again put out for tender in 2006.

Both ships have been responsible for minor oil spills. However, as the Lagoon is the Island's gateway to the open sea and a vital shipping trade, environmental watch-dogs, and their trainers, might be better off investing their finances, time and energy into building a 700 km bridge so that fuel can be trucked to the Island, and avoid such spills in the still pristine Lagoon.

Lord Howe Island Jetty

23

MORSE CODE TO MOTOR CARS

First Post Office

Courtesy of LHI Historical Society

Stan Fenton

THE POST OFFICE

In March 1852 a mailbag was found on Lagoon beach. Bound for London from Melbourne via Singapore, it was despatched on the ship *Jenny Lind* which was subsequently wrecked on Kenn's Reef off Queensland in September 1851. When the captain of the whaler *Jane* delivered the bag to the Sydney GPO, some of the mail was found to be still quite legible. Although mailbags are not in the habit of washing ashore today, messages in bottles are occasionally found on the Island beaches. And, sometimes they take less time than the mail to reach Lord Howe! Early in May 2005, a message written on 14 April was found in a barnacle encrusted bottle at Old Gulch. The bottle had been cast adrift from Ontong Java in the Solomon Islands!

Bill Nichols, his children Stan, Ron and Marion, and their horse, Jim

As the Island's honorary Postmaster from 1861, Captain William Spurling was entrusted with the collection and delivery of mail off the small trading vessels operating from Sydney. As the first officially appointed Postmaster in 1879, Captain Armstrong incurred the Islanders' disapproval when he refused to continue delivering the mail. After his dismissal in 1882 his successor, Campbell Stevens, reinstated the service and continued as Postmaster until 1924 when total deafness forced his retirement. The post office was then transferred to the home of Harry Smythe (married to Elsie Wilson), now Pandanus.

In 1929 a communications office was established from which all postal services were conducted. Stan Fenton (second son of Alexander and Mary) was appointed postmaster and OIC of the 'wireless station', the latter position he held until 1968. Stan developed an interest in radio operation as a child when he was taught morse code by Robert Baxter. He later trained as an operator with AWA. On 19 August 1929 he sent the first telegram in morse code from the Island. He remained postmaster until 1948 when the service was transferred to the home of Charlie Retmock (eldest son of William and Mary), now Mary Challis Apartments. After Charlie's death in 1959 a post office was built on a portion of John Thompson's lease, now Humpty Mick's café. John jnr (only son of John and Isabella) ran the service until his death in 1969. Several Islanders have since operated the post office, which is now in the hands of Peter Phillips (married to Janine, daughter of Barry and Marie Thompson). And the office is once again housed in the old wireless station building.

The bulk of incoming mail is delivered by sea freight from Yamba on a fortnightly basis. Airmail is subject to aircraft weight allowance. Although the mail service today has vastly improved from the 6-weekly deliveries of a by-gone era, it is still sometimes a source of frustration. Incoming mail is regularly misdirected to Norfolk or the Solomon Islands. In the latter there is a group of islands also named Lord Howe Island, but are locally known as Ontong Java!

DEPARTMENT OF CIVIL AVIATION

During World War II the Island played an important role in the collection and transmission of meteorological data, and in monitoring aircraft movement across the Pacific. In 1938 two large directional navigation towers, that still stand at the junction of Neds Beach Road and Anderson Road, were built by the Department of Civil Aviation. The Department took control of the wireless station, upgraded it, and installed a radio telephone, which enabled voice communication with aircraft over a limited range. The building was sandbagged and manned 24 hours a day. A coastal watch was maintained on Malabar, and an emergency transmitter was hidden on

Transit Hill. On one occasion Jim King (son of Ned and Janet), a regular look-out on Malabar, swore he spotted a submarine. Whether it actually was the enemy, or a whale, was not determined. The Island's closest encounter of the war kind came in 1946, when an anti ship mine washed ashore on Middle Beach and had to be detonated.

After the war, the Department of Civil Aviation's role was retained. Included in its duties were the safe operation of the flying boat service, reticulation of mains power around the Island, and the running of the telegraphy office. In 1975 it became the Department of Transport and included the Flight Service Office. On 11 August that year the last telegram was sent from the Island by the OIC, Rupert Giles. It was the last morse public correspondence circuit to be used in Australia. The Department of Transport ceased operation on the Island in 1989.

In its 50-year service, the Department gave employment to several Islanders – Harry Woolnough (married to Daisy Thompson) and his son Wallace, Fred Davies (married to Elsie Thompson), Norm Simpson (son of John and Ivy, nee Thompson) and John Green (son of Ozzie and Jean 'Bootie', nee Payten). It was also a source for local gossip when other Islanders joined employees for smoko in the amenities room, known as 'the Kremlin'.

THE METEOROLOGICAL STATION

Rainfall readings commenced on the Island in 1886, and records of climatological data began the following year. Observations were taken by a succession of residents until 1939 including Campbell Stevens, William Thompson and Edith Kirby.

The Meteorological Bureau shared the two-room wireless station from 1939 until 1955, when an independent station was completed on the eastern side of the Island above Middle Beach. Eight Island residents were employed to build the 'Met' under the supervision of a Sydney appointed foreman, Bill McGee (McGee's Parade so named). Work on the project was soon interrupted when they ran out of gravel needed for the cement footings. In fear of losing their lucrative employment while waiting on further supplies from the mainland; the 'gang of eight' hatched a plan to source the material from the base of treacherously steep cliffs at a site aptly named Hells Gate. In a task that McGee deemed too dangerous and could not be done; they achieved the 'impossible' by erecting a flying-fox, with Wally Wilson's horse, Girlie, providing the motive power.

The new facility was state-of-the-art at the time. It had a 277F S-band radar and an AWA 72 MHz radiosonde ground station. In addition, a voice radio link was established between Lord Howe and Sydney airport. The station was capable of radar weather surveillance out to a maximum range of 445 kms. Eventually it became the southernmost station in the cyclone tracking network.

Power was essential to the station's operation. The Department of Civil Aviation had its own works program at the time of the new construction. Apart from upgrading radio equipment, a new power station was being installed that would more than meet the requirements of both Departments. Consequently surplus power was made available to the Board. By 1955 all houses on the Island had electric lighting and were allowed to run a refrigerator. Prior to that time, guest houses and several private homes had installed their own power generators.

The provision of Met staff residences initially proved difficult; and mainland employees were forced to find temporary quarters until the houses were built. The prefabricated Riley Newson homes were shipped from Sydney on two vessels in September 1952. One ship arrived with a modest assortment of parts for the three homes, while the greater part of the consignment was carried on MV *Awahou*. About 150 kms south of the Island, that ship foundered and was lost with all hands. Further, when the *Jacques del Mar* washed onto the reef in 1954 the only cargo left on her to unload was Commonwealth property including VHF transmitters, drums of fuel, telegraph poles, copper cable and parts of the Met homes.

As the adverse weather conditions continued, the boat crew normally employed to work the ships refused to go near the wreck unless they were given complete salvage rights. This was not acceptable to the powers concerned and, in a 5-day operation, the salvage work was successfully undertaken by Commonwealth employees living on the Island.

Daily operation of the Met Station commenced at 2.30 am ceasing at 10.00 pm; except when flying boats were scheduled to depart Sydney before 5.00 am. On these occasions it was manned the full 24 hours. The staff consisted of three Observers and one Senior Radio 'tech' Observer. Mainland staff were employed on 3-year terms while Islander Mick Nichols was the only long-term employee. He received on-Island training as an Observer in 1939 and remained with the Bureau until his retirement in 1971. After the airstrip was constructed, the need to collect more accurate data for aircraft led to the relocation of the station in November 1988; to its present site near the airport.

A focal point of the Met Station's operation for tourists is the daily release of the weather balloons. They witness the take-off but never the landing. However, on 8 March 2004 they observed both. The morning balloon reached a height of 110,000 feet before bursting and descending to earth. Normally the upper wind structure is such that the balloons are taken away to the east (by the strong westerly winds aloft) and land in the ocean some 50 to 100 kms away. On this day the balloon travelled approximately 30 kms to the east before being blown back by easterly winds above 50,000 feet. When the balloon burst, a rapid descent landed it on the golf course – about 500 m away from where it was released two and a half hours earlier!

TELEPHONES

In 1975 the Department of Transport, through Telecom, supplied a direct telephone link between the Island and the mainland. Access was provided at the Post Office for a few hours a day Monday to Friday when Department traffic permitted. The postmaster, Garry Petherick (son of Russell and Joyce, nee Wilson), would travel by motorbike to residents' homes to advise them of incoming calls. The post office grounds became the daily social centre as locals wiled away their time waiting their turn in the *very* public telephone box – dubbed 'the confessional'! A telephone service through a manual exchange was installed in 1982. Direct dialling and television reception via satellite became possible with the advent of the AUSSAT satellite. Today, the only service not available is mobile telephones.

THE LOCAL PRESS

For several years after Stan's appointment as postmaster, Islanders were kept informed of outside and local events in *News of the World*. The two page paper, typed out by Stan three times a week, was posted on notice boards at the wireless station, Pinetrees and Ocean View.

Stan met competition when Cecil Whiting (son of William and Sue) opened a business on a portion of George Nichols' property. As a general goods outlet, it comprised an agency for the Bank of New South Wales, and a small room from which Cecil published the Island's first 'newspaper'. Beginning as a monthly paper distributed free to residents, its popularity grew to include visitors seeking them for souvenirs. Cecil then began asking a modest 3d per copy to cover paper and other costs. The demand grew but he refused to increase the charge, convinced that the newspaper was not worth more than 3d. Inevitably he lost money and abandoned the project in 1937.

In 1953, Jim Whistler (married to Lois Shick, granddaughter of John and Isabella Thompson) printed the first issue of *Signal*. For a short time he was assisted by Trevor Nixon, a retired commercial artist with the Sydney Morning Herald, who was a resident for five years. In 1987 *Signal* ceased publication and Daphne Nichols introduced the paper *Sail-O*. That venture lasted only a year and Jim then resurrected *Signal*. Today, it is published on a fortnightly basis and enjoys a reasonable mainland patronage for a small publication. After fifty years at the helm, Jim has handed editorship of *Signal* over to his assistant Barney Nichols (son of Mick and Norah).

TRANSPORT

The Island's first mode of transport were simple home-made bullock carts constructed of timber planks mounted on two axles, each with a 12-inch wheel at either end. Boxes were nailed to the platforms for seats. Sleds were made to carry seeds, freight and luggage. Horses or steers provided the power. Later, a charabanc comprising three rows of six seats was maintained by the Board as a community vehicle.

Bicycles were introduced shortly after World War I. For the young men of the day, they were something of a status symbol. While the best automobile attracted the ladies in the city, it was the best bike on Lord Howe! The competition was fierce, and their prized vehicles were identified by such names as Mountin' Rider, Pedal Prowler, Spoken For, Double Up and Nightie (easy to lift)! Alec Innes temporarily gained an edge when he imported the first motor bike in the late 1920s. However, after he sustained injuries in an accident the vehicle was removed.

By 1954 the Island's automotive transport comprised five vehicles of which three were owned by the Board: -

An ex-army 4wd blitz buggie to service the Department of Civil Aviation's installations

A small Ford Prefect sedan, owned by the doctor

A 1920s Thornycroft truck, converted from rubber on steel to pump up tyres

A post WW11 Bedford flat bed truck, also used as a community vehicle and tourist 'bus'

A Fordson tractor

Shortly after, Herbert Brearley's home made, 'Sound Barrier' became a novelty for the children as they watched it chug along the Island's roads.

At first the Board actively discouraged the use of privately owned vehicles, a policy that was vigorously fought by Gerald Kirby and other Islanders entering the tourist

146

industry when the flying boat service began. From that time, the increase in vehicle ownership was gradual until well after construction of the airstrip.

Today, the number has exceeded 200, and includes lodge operated buses, tour buses, hire cars, Board vehicles, trailers, motorbikes and privately owned cars. There is no public transport, although several years ago Bill and Pam Goyen (daughter of Wally and Dot Wilson) attempted a bus service but it proved unprofitable. Although the issue has become a major cause for concern, protagonists for 'no more' cars are mostly those who already possess a vehicle; and mainland groups who forget that the Island community's needs are similar to their own – but without such services as garbage collection, mail delivery or airport shuttle buses. In a recent local survey to garner public opinion on the motor vehicle question, 90% of the respondents thought there were too many, yet 93% claimed they would still need their own car if public transport became available!

Vehicle importation is subject to application through the Board and, given the 25 kph speed limit on the Island's roads, size and power are conditions attached to any approval. A policy was in place restricting households to one car and one motorbike – guest lodges were permitted more. However, the increasing population has resulted in a greater demand for vehicles; and a limit to the number the Island can sustain has not been fully addressed. The Board has now placed a moratorium on further importation, except for replacement vehicles, which are approved on a 'one on-one off' basis. A Vehicle and Traffic Advisory Group has been established to consider the issues pertaining to vehicle usage, and advise the Board on the development of a management plan.

This task could prove daunting given the genuine specific needs for vehicles – and the Government endorsed proposal for future residential development.

Bullock cart, early 1900s

147

24

IN SICKNESS AND IN HEALTH

In 1876 Surgeon T Corrie found that the population of Lord Howe Island appeared in good health, despite there being no doctor or hospital facilities. Aloe and castor oil plants, introduced by Dr Foulis in 1843; and Epsom salts seemed to be the curatives of all ailments. When Captain Armstrong's request for further medicines was rejected by the Government he found, according to his testimony to the 1882 Inquiry into his administration, that *a little colonial wine and brandy* offered relief to residents suffering from any kind of illness. After the Inquiry, the community medicine chest was increased to include: -

> 2 bottles carbonate ammonia; 1 bottle ether sulphur, one do. castor oil; 1 ullage bottle chlorodyne, one roll lint; 1 roll plaster, one pair tweezers, two lancets; 1 package needles, two pair forceps; 1 skein silk, one box camel-hair brush; 1 bottle seal volatile, one do. Epec. Wine; 1 package rhubarb pills, one parcel borax; 1 bottle soap liniment, 1 bottle pul. Epecac; 1 bottle Dover, one pot cerat. Flav. Resin; 1 bottle liquid epispasticas, one do. paregoric; 1 bottle Goulard's extract; 2 packages Steedman's soothing powders; 1 small piece oil-silk; 1 bottle extract ergot, one pair scissors; 1 part bottle myrrh aloes

William Clarson, who had a short teaching career on the Island in 1882, in his book *The Island of Lord Howe: the Madeira of the Pacific,* wrote of the Islanders: -

> Sickness is almost unknown, and the usual ailments are treated successfully without the aid of a doctor of any kind. No such thing as scarlet fever, small-pox, or other zymotic disease, except measles, which some years ago was introduced by a passing ship, has been known, and the presence of rheumatism is only to be attributed to indiscreet exposure while working during wet weather, and the entire neglect of any precaution to ward off colds and their complicated consequences.

The robust health and longevity of most of the first settlers was in stark contrast to the infant mortality rate that struck a third generation. The most common causes of death given in the Island's Register of Births, Death & Marriages were thrush, bronchitis, whooping cough, pneumonia, measles and convulsions induced by fever or infections (the main killer of babies under 12 months). The time these illnesses took to claim young lives was not long. Some died within a few days, while others succumbed in just a matter of hours. The tragedies were even more heartfelt when a family lost more than one child. One such case was Anne Robbins who died at '3 years, 10 months and 17 days' on 26 April 1885. Then on 15 August her parents, John and Mary, lost their 7-day old son.

William and Hannah Nichols had twelve children. They had lost six at the time of their youngest child's birth in 1897. However, the surviving children lived long and healthy lives. Ernest 'Tippy' Nichols, when asked what he attributed his good health to, replied it was *just enough Epsom salts each day to cover a sixpence.*

In July and August 1907, Emeline and Phyllis Dignam, known as 'Topsy' and 'Wacky', succumbed to whooping cough. The daughters of Phillip and Emeline, they were just 5 and 6 years old and died within two weeks of each other.

There were quite possibly many miscarriages but, considering the large families and the many years of active childbearing, it was to the credit of the 'four Marys' that not a mother or child were lost during complicated childbirths. Mary Nichols, Mary Wilson, Mary Robbins and Mary Fenton were all trained in midwifery by T B Wilson. However, it was said that in one incident before turning a breeched baby, Mary Nichols secured the mother's permission in writing via the magistrate; so that there would be no repercussions if the manoeuvre was unsuccessful.

Death did not visit infants alone. William and Lena Thompson had eleven children. After the loss of their youngest child in infancy, they suffered the ordeal of losing four grown children. Macey was 24 when he died from injuries sustained in a bicycle accident; Alice was 21 when she died from blood poisoning; Kenneth was 20 when he died from respiratory failure; and Larry was 30 when he lost his life in World War II.

From that time it would be many years before the Island lost young ones. Raylee Nobbs was an infant when she died from poisoning in 1959. Kim Morris (son of Richard and Monnie, nee Austic) lost his life in an accident in 1967 at the age of 20. A point on Malabar known as Kims Lookout bears his name.

During the 1920s and 1930s, several doctors and other professionals were residents of the Island for short periods. Among them were Thomas Brockhoff, Dr Mackay and Dr Deerberg. Living at Whitings, and in tents pitched on Austic's property, they were supposedly recovering from tuberculosis; although it was often said they were simply 'drying out'. Dr Deerberg was the only one Islanders believed really had the disease because of the 'spittle box' he constantly carried with him. However, while recuperating from whatever ailed them, they offered medical assistance in emergency situations. On one such occasion an operation was carried out on Phil Dignam's kitchen table, with a sterilized pen knife serving as a scalpel.

Visiting dentists plied their trade in the 'torture chamber', a small shed on George Nichols' land. After his death in 1947 the shed was moved to the home of Fred and Elsie Davies to house their power generator. Today, the property belongs to their daughter Joy, and the shed can still be seen in the bush behind Joys Shop.

In 1926 the Board of Control specified that the wives of appointed school masters should be double certificated nursing sisters who, in the absence of visiting doctors, were capable of maintaining the community dispensary, making professional calls and administering anaesthetic. This led to Nurse Lee and Nurse Folks providing medical services during their husbands' terms as teachers. Soon after Nurse Folks was appointed, her sister Doris Cameron arrived to give assistance. In 1940, Doris became the wife of Wally Wilson, son of Herbert and Harriett.

On 25 April 1941 the Gower Wilson Memorial Hospital was opened. Dedicated to the memory of Gower, his son Jack, William Hamill and three other crew members who perished on the *Viking* in 1936, the hospital was funded and built largely by the Islanders. Following its construction, the Hospital Womens Auxilliary played a major role in raising funds for equipment. A residence was built on the site once occupied by William and Mary Retmock and accommodated a succession of short-term doctors until 1949. Dick Browne was then appointed and remained on the Island for the next 24 years. He was followed by Ken Hicks and John Blythe. The current doctor, Frank Reed, has been in residence for nearly ten years. Two nurses assist in staffing the hospital; of which one position is held by Islander Karen Giles.

Once the responsibility of the Board, the hospital is now a multi purpose facility funded and administered by the South Eastern Sydney and Illawarra Area Health Service. Throughout the year, services are made available by visiting specialists in a number of fields. Outside community assistance for the elderly is also provided by the Home Care Service of NSW. Although the 4-bed hospital, which includes a dental surgery, is not equipped to deal with emergencies, the NSW Air Ambulance Service is readily available during daylight hours. In the event of life threatening situations, medical evacuations (once performed by Catalinas) are provided by RAAF Hercules, the only aircraft permitted night time use of the airstrip. Since 1974 several Islanders have been grateful to the RAAF.

The first evacuation was made by a Caribou on 4 August 1974. On that day, Wing Commander David Middleton was to captain the aircraft for a test landing on the partly finished airstrip, but the flight was cancelled due to strong westerly winds at the Island. However, when the RAAF learned that Wally Wilson had sustained serious injuries in an accident, Commander Middleton decided to make a mercy flight. Weather conditions deteriorated and wind gusts reached 70 knots from the south-west but, after five attempts, the Caribou made a safe landing. Wally was evacuated and made a complete recovery.

Health care has come a long way since the days of a glass of colonial wine, Epsom salts, the torture chamber and Phil Dignam's kitchen table!

25

RELIGION

Church of England services were originally conducted by a number of residents including Captain Spurling, Captain Tom Nichols (when he was not at sea), Campbell Stevens and J B Waterhouse. Occasionally, brief visits were made by clergymen travelling to Norfolk Island or the New Hebrides.

The first church, built of palm thatch with a biscuit barrel serving as a pulpit, was situated south of Windy Point in an area then known as Church Paddock. Today, the site forms part of the Special lease owned by siblings Garth and Daphne Nichols. On 27 February 1881 it was destroyed by a fire believed to have been lit by Isaac Mosely, who had a penchant for burning off wooded areas to extend his gardens. This particular fire blazed out of control and was not extinguished until it had spread north of Church Paddock, engulfing the little chapel on its way. Services were then held in the schoolhouse.

Adventism's first contact with Lord Howe Island was in September 1894. Pastor John Cole was travelling from Norfolk Island to Sydney on the *Oscar Robinson*, when unfavourable weather forced the vessel to stop at Lord Howe. During the 2-week delay, the Irish/American befriended Nathan Thompson and introduced Adventism to residents. When Pastor Cole reached Sydney, he requested that a missionary be sent to the Island. Charles and Beatrice Baron were chosen for the position, arriving in December 1894. Nathan offered them a small piece of his farm at the southern end of the Island; and church headquarters provided £120 for the construction of a small home. Besides providing scriptures, Pastor Baron offered free tuition to the children until his departure in 1897. However, his ministry was not immediately replaced and the congregation drifted back to the Church of England teachings.

In 1911, Mary Nichols met Pastor Arthur Ferris while on a visit to Norfolk Island. She was so impressed by him that she invited him to Lord Howe. He arrived in December that year but, after conducting several sermons, illness forced his return to Norfolk. However, after church headquarters noted that seven Islanders wished to convert to Adventism, Pastor Cecil Meyers was appointed in his place. He was not at all popular and residents, including Mary Nichols, grew antagonistic towards him. The interest in Adventism cooled, Meyers left, and the believers once again turned to the Church of England.

Interest developed again when a year later Pastor Edwin Butz was appointed. The first three Islanders to accept Adventism were baptised at Soldiers Creek on 27 February 1913. However, the baptism of Janet King was delayed a week, when her husband Ned threatened physical violence if she went ahead with the ceremony. But, by the end of March, Pastor Butz had baptised five more converts and when his replacement arrived in August that year, a third of the Islanders had embraced Adventism.

This so alarmed the Church of England that in 1914 their first mainland Minister was appointed. The Reverend A. Schapira, who was suffering from cancer, stayed only a year and was followed by Reverend Tranmer. He also retired within a year because of illness. T B Wilson was then appointed lay preacher, a position he held until 1920.

In 1914 the Board of Control allocated a portion of land for church purposes, of which half was secured by the Church of England. Construction of their church began in 1916. At the same time a site was selected for a rectory which, when T B resigned, was ready to accommodate Reverend Clark Kennedy in 1920. The site is today the home of Bill Thompson (son of Percy and Margaret). During Pastor Sid Nobbs' ministry, the Adventists claimed their half of the apportioned area and a Seventh Day Adventist church was completed in 1920. When Arthur Ferris returned that year for a second ministry, that would span fifteen years, Ellen Fenton offered a piece of land for a residence. Today it is the site of Capella Lodge.

When the Lord Howe Island Act was passed in 1953, a new site near Middle Beach Road was designated for church use. The Seventh Day Adventist Church and attached house opened in 1960, followed by the Anglican Church and rectory in 1961.

The Island also supports a Catholic community. At first, they relied on visiting priests and use of Government House to hold Mass. Then in the early 1990s, St Agnes' Catholic Church, with its residential annexe, took its rightful place next to the other churches, in what could now be called 'Church Paddock'.

FROM SEEDERS TO SOLDIERS

Roley Wilson, Carl Fenton, Gower Wilson, Phil Brack, Norm King,
Harold Nichols, Nathan Thompson

The outbreak of the Great War was somewhat of a shock to Mary Nichols who, as an ardent fan of 'Kaiser Bill', proudly displayed his photograph in her living room. However, when nine of Lord Howe Island's strapping young seeders put down their cubbies and enlisted in the Australian Infantry Forces, Mary begrudgingly took down the picture of her German king.

Tom Innes and Harold Nichols, were Mary's grandsons. Tom was killed in action at Hangard Wood on the Somme in 1917. His mother Grace claimed she was clairvoyant and while resting one afternoon, she felt the presence of her son in the room. Believing he was saying goodbye, she called his siblings together to tell them Tom had died. However, official news of his death did not reach the Island until 14 June 1918. After the War, Harold became a Surveyor on the mainland during which time he was employed in the construction of the Sydney Harbour Bridge.

Arthur Dignam also made the supreme sacrifice. He died on a hospital train from wounds recieved in France in November 1916.

William Retmock, Gower and Roley Wilson (sons of T B and Mary), Norm King (son of Ned and Janet) and Nathan Thompson (son of William and Lena) returned to the Island after the War. Carl Fenton (son of Alexander and Mary) later joined the NSW Police Force.

In 1925 a sandstone memorial, dedicated to Tom and Arthur, was built in the Church of England grounds on Lagoon Road. Then in 1928 the foundations were laid for the Island's Cenotaph. Materials forming the support columns of the stone shelter were brought ashore from Blackburn Island. A World War I German MG08 machine gun, captured at Villers Bretonneux on 9 July 1918, was housed within the memorial.

Twenty-four men enlisted in the Forces during World War II, serving in Europe, North Africa, New Guinea, Singapore and the Solomons. Frank Payten (son of Henry and Mabel) had joined the Merchant Navy (Burns Philp) prior to the War breaking out.

Nathan and Roley were veterans of World War I. Larry Thompson (brother of Nathan) lost his life when he was shot down over Germany. Ron Payten (son of Harry and Mabel) spent three years as a POW in Changi.

Roy Wilson, Norm Fenton, Jack Williams, Fred Davies, John Thompson (son of John and Isabella), Eric Hines (son of Reg and Kathleen, nee Nichols), Bryant Smythe (son of Harry and Elsie) and Richard Morris (married to Monnie Austic) returned to the Island at the end of the War. Les King (son of Norm and Maggie, nee Hamill) remained in the Air Force until 1962.

Cecil Whiting, William, Fred and Bob Baxter (sons of Robert and Ethel), Percy Thompson (brother of Nathan and Larry), Tom Wilson (son of Herbert and Harriet), Ron Kirby (son of Gerald and Edith) and William Marlin (married to Halcyon Wilson) pursued careers on the mainland.

Henry Buffet, Arlie and Macey Quintal were Norfolk Islanders, who had been Lord Howe residents for a number of years. Henry and Arlie were killed in action.

Although only a small number picked up their seeding cubbies again, the climbing skills of Lord Howe Island seeders, in both wars, won them admiration among their peers — and many wagers!

Several Islanders joined the Defence Forces in peace time while others were called up for National Service. Esven Fenton (son of Norm and Lillian), Peter and Stan Fenton (sons of Stan and Elsie), Dean Retmock (son of Bill and Doreen) and Ashley Wilson (son of Terry and Shirley) served in the Air Force, Garth Nichols (son of Mick and Norah), Stephen Simpson (son of Norm and Daphne) and Ian Fitzgerald (son of Jim and Mavis) served in the Army. A promising career for Philip Crombie ended tragically

Tom Innes

when he was murdered in a park near Holsworthy Army base. Matthew Retmock (brother of Dean) also chose the Army as a career but was forced to resign on medical grounds. Max Shick (son of Jack and Gladys, nee Thompson), joined the Navy. Max's son Terry and Larry Wilson (son of Roley and Olive, nee Thompson) were called up for National Service. Kate Dignam (daughter of Carl and Fay) was in the Army Reserve.

Stan and Garth (Army artillery) served in Vietnam. Later, as an RAAF Squadron Leader, Stan participated in ferrying F-111's from the USA to Australia. He retired from the Air Force as a Wing Commander.

Other men who served in the three conflicts and are now long-term residents of the Island include Jim Lonergan, Dick Hoffman and Jamie Elliott (married to Betty, nee Woolnough).

THE RSL CLUB

The Lord Howe Island Sub-Branch of the Returned Servicemens League was formed in February 1947, followed by the RSL Womens Auxiliary in July 1948. Over the next few years, funds were raised through a variety of activities for a clubhouse. The RSL Club was officially opened by the Governor of NSW, Sir John Northcott on 14 May 1951. For the next 25 years the Club played host to visiting personnel from the armed forces; ran social functions and sponsored local events including an annual athletics carnival for the children. The Club was also the Friday evening 'local'; and the starting point for its members doing the 'rounds' of Island homes on Christmas mornings. In 1955 this festive season tradition was nearly not so festive when the Board, having established its liquor store at the Public Hall in the previous October, cancelled the Club's alcohol supply from the mainland store Bird's a week before Christmas!

In the mid 1970s, the small number of RSL members

Harold Nichols

decided a permanent clubhouse was no longer needed; and in 1978 the building was established as the Lord Howe Island Museum.

The first Anzac service was held in 1930 and is traditionally conducted by both the Anglican and the Seventh Day Adventist Church ministers. The Anzac Day march began in 1946 with ex-servicemen from both wars participating. Many of those veterans are deceased but younger generations, wearing the medals worn by their forefathers, now march in their place. The short procession from the Museum to the Cenotaph, takes them along Lagoon Road and under the arched gateway bearing the inscription:-

LEST WE FORGET

Laying the foundation for the war memorial, 1928

(unknown), Harold Clough, (unknown), Harry Smythe, Bill Marlin, Gower Wilson, William Retmock, (unknown), (unknown), Jack Shick, T C Douglass, Max Nicholls

27

DAYS AT ISLAND SCHOOL

Courtesy of LHI Historical Society

The Island School, 1922. Back Row: G M Kirby, Bob Baxter, Elsie Thompson (Davies), Will Baxter, Hilda Thompson (West), Cecil Whiting, Monnie Austic (Morris), Ron Kirby, Norm Fenton, Tom Wilson.

Front: Mick Nichols, Larry Thompson, Veronica Wilson (Thornton), Jack Wilson, Fred Baxter, Lena Thompson (Williams), Phyllis Nichols (Lyon), Eileen Wilson (Douglass).

Sporadic attempts to educate the early children of Lord Howe Island in 'reading, writing and arithmetic' were undertaken by Isaac Mosely, Captain Field and Captain Spurling. It was not until 1878 that positive action was taken to establish a proper school. On noting there were fifteen school age children, and another five or six older persons who expressed an interest in schooling, Captain Armstrong sought a more formal approach to education. After persuading T B Wilson to remain on the Island as a teacher, Captain Armstrong, in a letter to the Council for Education, wrote:-

> For the last eight months Mr Thomas B. Wilson, resident of the Island, has undertaken without remuneration, to give some of the children a few hours education daily and as he is well educated, and writes a good clerical hand and produces first class testimonials of past services, I would strongly recommend that he be appointed as Provisional Schoolmaster to the Island.

He was officially appointed on 29 July 1879 on a salary of £48 per annum. If the average attendance at the school exceeded fifteen pupils for any month, he could claim an additional £5; if it exceeded eighteen, an extra £6; and, if more than twenty-one pupils attended, he could claim another £7. The salary, paid by the Council, was to be augmented by school fees usually payable at the rate of 9d per week for one child, and 6d per week each for two or more children from the same family. However, as there was very little coin on the Island T B, if he was paid by the Islanders at all, was probably paid in farm produce.

The Council supplied the following articles: -

> 16 Scripture lessons from the New Testament and 12 from the Old Testament, 12 Supplement to Fourth Book of Lessons, 18 Constable's Education Reading Books, 12 Constable's Second English Reading Books, 21 Constable's Primer First Part Reading Books, 24 Australian Class Books, 1 Map of the World, 1 Map of the Western Hemisphere, 1 box of chalk, 1 ball frame and a quantity of lesson sheets.

After T B's resignation in May 1880 the school closed, despite Captain Armstrong's recommendations of two persons suited to the teaching position. Robert Rose, although approved by the Council in 1881, declined to accept because the Islanders disapproved of his association with the 'delinquent' Vernon boys. In May 1882 William Clarson's appointment was swiftly terminated when he fell foul of the law for committing bigamy.

Following the Inquiry into Captain Armstrong's administration in 1882, Commissioner Wilson reported to the Colonial Secretary, that: -

> Many of the inhabitants of the Island are to be praised for their individual exertions to educate their children, but now that a public school building has been erected it certainly is the duty of the Government to see that a competent master is kept on the Island, seeing that before the holidays twenty-nine children were on the roll and the daily average was twenty.

Subsequently in September 1882, William Stevens was appointed to the position and the school reopened. However, he found there were only *eight* children in attendance, and of that number some were not allowed to stay for the afternoons. He reported the average class attendance to be less than five pupils. By July 1883 it was determined that the Islanders cared little for schooling; and the £120 salary and £26 house allowance per annum would be better spent elsewhere. Again the school closed.

Magistrate Henry Wilkinson succeeded in reopening it in July 1884 when he advised the Colonial Secretary that there were *twenty* children on the Island. He recommended that William Stevens be reinstated adding that the conduct of Stevens and his wife, during his first term of employment, had a *beneficial influence on the general tone of the people*. The Magistrate's request was investigated, but it was found that only *six* children were of the ages to come within the compulsory clauses. Nevertheless, it agreed to reappoint Stevens. Once again attendances were poor and he blamed it on the apathy of the parents, commenting that it was a *waste of money* to continue his appointment. The school closed for the third time in May 1887.

Several attempts were made to reopen it between 1887 and 1890 including a proposal by Thomas Sharp, a private tutor, to run a night school. Celine Moore, a resident on the Island in 1889, applied for the position but was rejected on the grounds that she was living in sin; and had made a fraudulent application under the surname of her common law husband, Edmund Jeune. When they returned to Sydney, Celine, in a letter to Magistrate Icely, wrote: -

> Before leaving the island several of the inhabitants expressed the desire that I should be appointed school teacher there, and as far as I am personally concerned I should like to return. Will you kindly tell me if there is any likelihood of my being appointed if I apply. Mr Jeune and I were married on Saturday.

Her letter was passed on to the Department of Public Instruction who decided she was now qualified for the position. And, after Mary Nichols informed the Department that there were *nineteen* children between the ages of 6 and 14 who could now attend, the school reopened in February 1891. Celine was paid an advance in salary but then her appointment was rescinded. Instead, the position was granted to Mrs Cavage, whose husband was the newly appointed Forest Ranger on the Island. However, once again the children appeared to have vanished! Attendances were so low that the school closed in 1895. Soon after, the schoolhouse blew down in a gale. Pastor Baron rebuilt it and volunteered his services as a teacher until 1897.

After another attempt failed to reopen the school in 1901 the Chief Inspector from the Department of Education concluded that, through the *want of unanimity among the Islanders*, it would not be prudent to appoint another teacher or grant any aid to the Island for school purposes. Undaunted, the Islanders approached Magistrate Frank Farnell for assistance and, in 1902, the Government appointed George Massy Kirby as teacher. Education finally began in earnest and the school was no longer an 'open and shut case'!

Beginning with a class of sixteen children, George Kirby's career spanned twenty years. He introduced school uniforms – pinafores for the girls and shorts or knickerbockers (poop catchers) with shirt and tie for the boys. Shoes were not a prerequisite. Roll was called every morning and punctuality was a strict rule. Scripture started the school week when Mr Kirby read a passage from the bible. Besides reading, writing and arithmetic he taught geography, in which the counties of England, Ireland and Scotland; and the States of America were learned off by heart. The names of British monarchs and the years in which they reigned, formed the basis of his history lessons. Instead of pictures on the walls he hung testimonials from shipwrecked men, expressing their gratitude for the kindness the Islanders had shown them after they reached the safety of Lord Howe.

By 1916 there were twenty-two children enrolled. That year an Inspector from the Department of Education paid an informal visit to the Island and reported that Mr Kirby was: -

> a man of more than ordinary intelligence and ability, with a good secondary education and a wide and varied life experience. He possesses a large fund of general knowledge as well as a considerable degree of literary culture and 'savoir faire'

The Inspector also commented that: -

> the children are made the means of fulfilling kind neighbourly offices. Those who keep cows bring cans of milk to be taken home by those who have none, and so with fruit and other things. There is no barter, only mutual goodwill

The school continued in the charge of George Kirby; and under the administration of the Board until 1922. Financially weakened by the effects of World War I, and the impact of rats on the palm seed industry, it was forced to hand over responsibility for the school to the Department of Education. Mainland teachers were then appointed for one to five year terms, beginning with Clem Smith in 1923.

In 1949 when there were fifty students enrolled, the Department of Education appointed a second teacher. Further, in 1973 an enrolment of over sixty students prompted the appointment of a third teacher. This allowed the school to separate Infants, Primary and Secondary classes, with a separate teacher for each level. While the number of students today has decreased to forty, the mainland teaching staff remains the same with the added assistance of two casual positions filled by Islanders.

More than fifty teachers have passed through the Island school since the days of George Massy Kirby. Of that number, three made Lord Howe Island their home. Carol Browne married Neil Woolnough (son of Harry and Daisy); and Sue Rodger married Garth Nichols. The third teacher was a man whose name is synonymous with the Island to this day.

Max Nicholls was appointed in 1924. In his enthusiasm for teaching music, the lack of instruments was not a deterrent to forming a school band. Flutes, tin whistles, fiddles, banjos and drums, either bought or home-made, provided the music. He also encouraged craft lessons in which baskets, hats and mats were made from pandanus leaves. When his term expired, Max did not return to his native Tasmania. He continued to live in the Baxter home until 1948 when he moved to a small cottage on Mick Nichols' property. He remained there until his death in 1956. Today the cottage, known as Jeds Shack, is owned by Barney Nichols. Max gave violin lessons, and formed another school band during a second teaching term in 1942. As a keen student of natural history he pioneered many walking trails, including the track to North Bay that bears his name. Max's love of nature and the Island was reflected in his 1938 book *A History of Lord Howe Island*.

THE SCHOOL

The first schoolhouse was situated on a portion of land where the small cricket pitch is today. It was built by Captain Armstrong's kanakas who were to receive tuition in return for their labour. However, the building was considered too small. A request to the School Council for £80 to build a more suitable facility, which could also serve as a church, was approved and a new schoolhouse was completed at the end of 1881. Built by the residents, it blew down in a gale in 1895. Fortunately, it was during a 'closed' period so nobody was hurt! After it was rebuilt, it functioned for another thirty-two years before the Islanders successfully petitioned for a new school. The new building, on the site of the present school, was completed in 1927. The old schoolhouse was moved to a new site and used as a storeroom for palm seeds. When the Public Hall replaced it in 1936, Herbert Brearley purchased the old building for use as an engine and lumber room.

School House (1895-1927)

The running of the school was largely attributed to the Parents and Citizens Association, which was formed in 1937 during Austin Lee's teaching appointment. At first it was active in raising funds for the provision of school materials, sporting equipment and major items such as the contruction of a tennis court in 1949. When the Department of Education began supplying most school requisites, the Association's activities were then channelled into raising funds for school excursions and student participation in combined athletics events on the mainland.

World War II added new activities to the school curriculum. Besides normal lessons, the children prepared the school against enemy attack. Air raid trenches were dug in which they practiced getting to in a speedy yet orderly manner each day. They also planted gardens to assist in the war effort; proceeds from the sale of their crops going to the Australian Comfort Fund.

In 1949 the Department of Education decided that another classroom was needed to facilitate the increasing number of students. The Public Hall was used as an Infants' classroom during construction of the new building, on which the senior boys were assistant labourers. The Secondary classroom was officially opened by the Governor of NSW, Sir John Northcott, on 15 May 1951. From that time on, students felt a great sense of importance when they completed their Primary learning in the 'little school' and moved into the 'big school'.

When Harry Cairns was appointed principal in 1954 the annual athletics carnival, normally hosted by the RSL, was taken over by the school. Competition in the carnival was divided into two 'houses' aptly named Lidgbird and Gower. The sports and an annual swimming carnival (introduced in 1968) are still competed by students forming these two teams.

Shool uniforms were reintroduced during Maurie Reeve's appointment, having been abandoned after George Kirby retired. School badges accessorised the less formal attire, but footwear was still not a requirement.

A major upgrading of the school occurred in 1960 with the installation of a septic system toilet block. Although hygienically desirable, the children sorely missed the pit toilets. The long drops were their 'forts' which, hidden in the bush beyond the tennis court, were constantly defended in war games between the boys and the girls. The boys' fort was also the object for testing home-made bombs. Needless to say, not one of those boys ever became a scientist! However, for some unknown reason, the new toilets offered students the opportunity to excel in life – at least that was according to a visiting Department Officer who, after inspecting the facility, wrote: -

The new septic toilet and ablution block has been used to good educational advantage

Because of a high number of Secondary students, the school was reclassified as a Central School in 1966; and the provision of a separate building that contained the necessary facilities at secondary level was endorsed by the Department of Education. Funding was allocated and a science block was officially opened by the Governor of NSW, Sir Roden Cutler, on 16 February 1968. The new building and cement quadrangle replaced the tennis court.

During the School Centenary Celebrations in 1979 special guests included the

Governor of NSW, Sir Roden and Lady Cutler; the school's patron and Premier of NSW, Neville Wran and his wife Jill; the Minister for Education, Eric Bedford; and the NSW Director-General of Education, Doug Swan. And, of course, many ex-students and a number of teachers revisited their special place of learning.

While enrolments might not have increased dramatically over 126 years Lord Howe Island Central School, now a modern educational facility boasting the motto *Today for Tomorrow,* is a far cry from the little building that blew down in a gale in 1895.

THE STUDENTS

The frequent opening and closing of the school in the early years, through poor attendance, was perhaps unfairly blamed on the apathy of the parents. It is doubtful they understood the attendance ratio required in keeping a school open and while they wanted schooling for their children, money was scarce. The community's dependence on farming took priority over education. Further, there seemed little need for it when the Kentia Palm Seed industry's share system offered employment and security to all Island families. However World War I, and the decimation by rats to the seed crops, had a marked effect on the share system. With their security in jeopardy, Gerald Kirby actively encouraged students to further their education on the mainland. By the early 1950s, even after the introduction of correspondence learning, most students were completing their secondary education at boarding schools. Also, for some years after air services began in 1974 free student air travel with Oxley Airlines, and billeted accommodation, afforded educational opportunities at Port Macquarie High School.

From 1932, Blackfriars Correspondence School (1924-1990) offered schools in remote areas of NSW special courses for secondary education to the Leaving Certificate level; and later the Higher School Certificate. However, this assistance was not readily available to Lord Howe Island until the flying boats provided a regular mail service. When Blackfriars closed in 1991 the decentralised provision of Distance Education commenced. Although this system supports those students who wish to complete their secondary education on the Island; many still prefer the interaction and resources found in larger mainland schools.

With their school years behind them, many ex-students remained on the Island; some to become successful tourist and business operators. Others followed a diversity of careers on the mainland.

Several were offered opportunities abroad. During their careers with the Bank of New South Wales (now Westpac), Bob Baxter was transferred to a management position in

163

London; while Barney Nichols spent several years as an officer in New Guinea. After being crowned Miss Australia in 1960, Rosemary Sinclair forged a career in Public Relations with the same Bank. In 1967 she was appointed Australia's Chief Hostess at Expo in Canada. Rosemary later co-founded NAPCAN (National Association for the Prevention of Child Abuse and Neglect). While stationed in Singapore with the RAAF in the 1950s, Les King was selected to the Australian Services cricket team for their matches against state sides, including the NSW Sheffield Shield champions. Phillip Whistler (son of Jim and Lois), a Radiologist, is also a keen sportsman who has competed in Iron-Man events in Hawaii and New Zealand. Adrian Skeggs (son of Ray and Celia, nee Austic) is an ex-wallaby who coached rugby union overseas. Sean Lonergan (son of Jim and Betty, nee Woolnough) is based in Hong Kong as a Captain with Dragon Airlines. After graduating from Sydney University with degrees in Science and Medicine, Russell Williams (son of Alan and Lena) furthered his career in the USA, where he still resides. His sister, Cheryl, spent some years nursing in England and Europe; while Lorraine de Rusett (daughter of Fred and Elsie Davies) and Patricia Dignam nursed in Canada and the USA respectively. Patricia's brother, Arthur, is a renowned stage and screen actor whose talents took him to London. Rhonda Wilson (daughter of Roley and Olive) was a teacher in England; and Diane Owens (daughter of Roy and Daphne Wilson) taught in Zimbabwe. Lance Wilson (son of Herbert and Lillian), John Wilson (son of Allen and Eve, nee Smythe), Terry Shick (son of Max and May) and Stuart King (son of Les and Dulcie) travelled extensively in the course of their merchant navy careers.

Although the population and businesses have increased, opportunities are still limited and, as such, many of the younger Islanders still continue to seek careers on the mainland.

Irrespective of the different paths taken, generations of students have fond memories of their barefoot days at Island school. In just over a century the school uniform has evolved to include a hat – but still no shoes. Although footwear is now a fashion statement in some quarters *outside* school; shoes have long been considered an inconvenience, deemed necessary only when visiting the 'big smoke'. On one such occasion, Beth Kirby, while in Sydney with her young daughters, noticed Jenny was in an agitated state. Upon asking what was upsetting her, Jenny replied: -

> I just wanna go home to me own country and take me shoes off

Lord Howe Island School, 2005

Back: Ian Lucas (Principal)

Fourth Row: Bronwyn Tofaeono (Teacher), Lauren Taafe, Bonnie Whitfield, Seanna Makiiti-Young, Rhyenn Buckley, Taylah Young, Luke Delarue, Georgia Shick, Laura Goyen, Melissa Borsato (Teacher)

Third Row: Jenny Foster (Teacher), Jack Buckley, Bronte Phillips, Nelson Retmock, Ruby Charlton Shick, Daniel Kennedy, Bianca Fitzgerald, Vincent Kennedy, Ella Taafe, Harrison Brus, Chloe Delarue, Rhonda Wilson (Teacher)

Second Row: Tom Kelly, Brooke Busteed, Madison Gardiner, Stephen Sia, Marnie Young, Luke Wright, Jessie-Rose Krick, Nathan Retmock, Natalie Wilson, Kayla Hiscox, Matthew Wilson

First Row: Mitchell Nobbs, Anna Charlton Shick, Tyrin Thompson, Charlotte Tofaeono, Noah Busteed, Gina Krick, Jayden Hiscox, Sarah Wilson, Aaron Pottage, Abbey Phillips

165

28

FOR THE LOVE OF SPORT

Mick Nichols and Stan Fenton

From rudimentary games of cricket and rounders in the late 1800s, a rifle range at Old Settlement in the 1940s, to today's touch footy, Islanders have always embraced sporting activities and the interaction they have offered between the young and older generations. Their abilities and sportsmanship are reflected at the annual Discovery Day Sports Carnival, initiated by Jim Whistler more than thirty years ago.

THE CRICKET CLUB

Cricket became the first organised sport after Henry Wilson introduced the game to the Island in the 1870s. Bats and stumps were fashioned from Island timber while Bill Brown made cricket balls out of sennet. With the assistance of cricket enthusiast Magistrate Frank Farnell, a Club was finally formed in August 1900. William Dignam was the elected President. The designated area for play was cleared of scrub and by 1901 it was an established cricket ground, named Farnell Park in honour of the Club's Patron. At a meeting in October that year, black and gold were chosen as the playing colours; and an annual fee was set at 2/6d for adults and 1/- for boys under sixteen. However, after Farnell retired in 1910, interest in play dwindled and lack of funds forced the Club to close. There was a renewed interest after World War I and the Club reopened in November 1922; with an annual fee fixed at 12/-. By the early 1930s its financial position enabled players to compete against visiting teams and enter competition matches in Sydney and at Norfolk. Cricket became so popular that all industry ceased for the Friday afternoon games.

As lawn bowls grew in popularity, interest in cricket as a competitive sport again waned and the clubhouse, situated in the western corner of the ground, was eventually demolished. However social matches are still played against tourists, yachtsmen competing in the Gosford to Lord Howe Island race, and visiting navy personnel.

THE BOWLING CLUB

In 1922, at the instigation of Harry and Phil Payten, the Board of Control granted a portion of land on which the Lord Howe Island Bowling Club was formed. William Thompson was elected foundation President. Hector Ross, a resident for a number of years, gave a garden shed that was upgraded to serve as a clubhouse. He later donated a roller and top dressing plant. Two visitors by the name of R Nall and M Carle donated bowls and £5 each towards the upkeep of the club. The 4-rink green opened in 1923.

The War years, and Harry Payten's death in 1945, saw a decline in the game and the green and clubhouse fell into disrepair. However, in 1954 moves to reopen it were supported by Robert Baxter, Mick Nichols, Stan Fenton, Dick Browne and Arthur Sainsbury (married to Ilma Hines). It opened in 1955 with Jim Cunningham (second husband of Ivy Thompson), elected as President. Renovations and extensions funded largely by members were carried out in 1960. The new building was officially opened by the Governor of NSW, Sir Eric Woodward. Major renovations were again undertaken in 1992.

The introduction of airline services afforded entry to mainland tournaments and inter-island competitions with Norfolk Island. However, after the collapse of Norfolk Airlines in 1991 the latter competitions were difficult to maintain. In February 1976 the Club hosted the Supply Fours, its first regular open tournament. For several years, as part of this event, competing RAAF teams from Richmond challenged local teams for the Administrator's Trophy. The Supply Fours are now played every four years as part of the Quadrangular Series, hosted on a rotational basis by Lord Howe, Norfolk, NSW and the ACT. Lord Howe Island teams won the tournament in Queanbeyan in 2005, and on home ground in 2006.

The Tasman Triples, another major tournament, is hosted in November and is keenly contested by mainland teams. Local club events are played regularly, and like cricket in the early years, industry all but ceases for social bowls on Thursday afternoons.

TENNIS

Although a club was never officially established, for many years tennis formed a big part of the sporting and social scene, and courts dotted the settlement area. The first, built on George Nichols' property in the early 1900s, was followed by courts at Pinetrees, Thompson's paddock, the School and Ocean View. Three still exist and social games are played on a regular basis.

THE SAILING CLUB

Phil Payten founded the Sailing Club in 1937; its members electing John Thompson snr as Commodore and Herbert Wilson as President. Races were divided into two classes – 'A' class for boats over 12 ft, and 'B' class for boats 12 ft and under. By 1938 there were fourteen boats ranging from 24 ft to 12 ft on the Club's register. Sailing races were held every Sunday and many of the sailing teams were made up of women.

The sport was interrupted when many of the Island's young men left to serve in World War ll. After the war several veterans remained on the mainland, and the Club eventually ceased operation. Attempts to reestablish sailing as a competitive sport were made by a number of school teachers and public servants in the 1970s and 1980s, when the Aquatic Club was formed. The Club today is active in arranging weekend recreational sailing.

THE GOLF CLUB

Le-Toa Golf Links was established by Frank 'Cobby' Robbins (son of John and Mary) in the late 1950s. Once the site of his father's garden, the 9-hole course has been developed and expanded into one of the most picturesque and challenging golf courses in Australia. The first clubhouse was situated in Frank's former house at Cobbys Corner, now the home of Judy Wilson (second wife of Wally). The present clubhouse was the residence of Ron and Celia Farrar (daughter of Cobby and Amy, nee Nobbs), and in the early days of golf it accommodated the Club's greens keeper.

A series of local competitions and weekly social events lead up to the Golf Open Tournament in November. This event attracts a large number of mainlanders, many of whom have competed since its inception fourteen years ago. Several Islanders have won this tournament.

THE GOSFORD TO LORD HOWE ISLAND YACHT RACE

In 1972 Gosford yacht owners, Peter Rysdick and Lloyd Pryke, visited the Island on a pleasure cruise. They were taken by the beauty of the Island and the hospitality of its residents. The idea for an annual yacht race and a perpetual trophy crystallised one night over dinner at Pinetrees when Beth Kirby told Peter and Lloyd: -

> I will give you a fine perpetual trophy if you organise the race

The inaugural Gosford to Lord Howe Island Yacht Race commenced the 420 nautical mile race in late October 1973, under the auspices of the Gosford Aquatic Club (now Gosford Sailing Club). Awaiting the winner *Helsal* was the Pinetrees trophy Beth Kirby promised. The unique piece of silverware was originally a perpetual trophy for the Penang Turf Club in Singapore in its colonial days. The cup is now one of the most sought after trophies in Australian yacht racing.

Because of the Island's unique environment, the keenly contested lead up to the Sydney-Hobart Race is now limited to 22 boats. However thirty-two years after its inception, and despite moves by Sydney yacht clubs to take it over, the Gosford-Lord Howe race, now a yachting classic, remains an outstanding ocean racing event, organised and run by Gosford yachtsmen.

During the 1980s a number of Islanders participated in this race, crewing on *Freight Train*.

FISHING

Whether a sporting or recreational activity, for 165 years this vital part of Lord Howe

Island's community had just one umpire – the weather! Once conducted from beaches, bays and rocks, many of the keen anglers were women. Several favourite sites still bear the names of those Islanders who first frequented them. Using lines made from the Kurrajong tree, and young muttonbirds or witchety grubs as bait, the first settlers fished for only what was required to feed their families. If more than the quota was caught, the surplus fish would be placed in rock pools for others without their share to take. Later, converted whaleboats and other craft were either rowed or sailed to various fishing locations. With the advent of diesel powered launches, fishing activities were extended to such offshore locations as the Pyramid, Wolf Shoal, South East Bank, South East Rock and Sunken Rock.

Over the years, small quantities of fish have been exported, beginning with a shark fishing cooperative in 1930. The Company, established by a mainlander, set up a processing unit on Blackburn Island for the export of skins to a Sydney manufacturer of fashion accessories. It ceased in 1931 when the Manager fleeced ten Island investors of their hard earned money and disappeared. During World War II, parcels of fish were sent to the mainland when a ship called in, and in recent years a small number of tuna was exported to the mainland and Japanese markets.

Although the tourist boom increased the demand for locally caught fish, the season is short; and the activity is still dictated by the predominantly adverse weather and sea conditions. Unlike the intrusion by long-liners into the waters surrounding the Island, locals have long respected the bans imposed on spear-fishing, fish-traps, the taking of certain species and fishing at Neds Beach. The latter is a fish feeding site and, although a keen fisherman, for many years Brian 'Karta' Simpson has been their feeder and custodian. In 1999 concern over the depletion in fish stocks, and the preservation of marine bio-diversity, brought another referee into the game. A 46,000 hectare Marine Park, and its legislation, has placed further restrictions on the Island's small industry. Commercial and recreational fishing have been minimised, while all fishing activity is banned in 27% of the total area. Several traditional fishing spots lie within the sanctuary zones.

WATER SPORTS

Many Islanders were fishing enthusiasts but few ventured into the water to swim. Norah Nichols was born in England and as a small child she learned to swim in the local pool. She was a strong swimmer long before she set eyes on the Pacific Ocean. Naturally, when Norah arrived at the Island in 1933, she was amazed at the number of residents who could not swim. When she asked fellow swimmer Aggie Christian (daughter of Alexander and Mary Fenton) the reason for it, Aggie's response was – *they think swimming scares away the fish.*

The Islanders have come a long way since then. During Harry Cairns' term as headmaster, the school had the distinction of winning the 1955 Bowen Cup for Lifesaving. This involved the senior students spending many hours of swimming and lifesaving practice in the Lagoon near the Far Rocks. Competing against mainland schools of up to three hundred pupils, it became the smallest school ever to win the trophy. Swimming has since become part of the school curriculum and a carnival is held annually.

The first surfboard on the Island, which was quite a novelty in 1957, was a 9-foot coral pink foam Malibu owned by the Nichols children. The next surfboard was owned by Stan Fenton. Today, almost everyone who enters the water owns a surfboard or multiples thereof. A local competition is held annually, and the breaks are jealously guarded from the outside world. Children learn their skills in Surfers Hole at Neds Beach, before venturing to such breaks known as Mexico, Grinder, Little Island, Little Reef, Half Moon, La Meurthe, Ulli and South Reef.

A cold and wet morning on 30 May 2002 did not deter David 'Harry' Rourke (son of Ed and Pixie) from checking out his favourite break at South Reef. If the conditions were good he would pass the news on to other surfers. Tragically, he died when his motorbike skidded off Lagoon Road into a tree. Soon after dawn on the day of his funeral, the surfing community gathered on a flotilla of boards at South Reef. They formed a circle and joined hands before riding a final wave in honour of their friend. Harry was laid to rest beside his grandfather, Gerald Kirby, in the Pinetrees cemetery. His favourite surfboard was buried with him. South Reef is now known by his mates as Harry's Reef.

Harry
(1972-2002)

171

THE EARLY SOCIAL SCENE

Castaways amused themselves by singing and dancing and at times there were forty sitting down to meals in groups of three. (Max Nicholls)

Nathan Thompson, besides celebrating his native country's Independence Day and Thanksgiving with American whalers, welcomed the community into his home every Christmas. Visitors were added to the guest list and it was said that the gatherings grew so large, it was not unusual for fifty or sixty to be served dinner from the 'festive board' each year. After Nathan's death, his family continued the tradition until the mid 1920s.

Mary Nichols often organised sing-a-longs; and later her party loving daughters, Edith, Martha and Sue, entertained Islanders and visitors alike at their many soirees. At these affairs their lace-dresses, long cigarette holders, crystal glassware and fine wine reigned supreme.

It was also customary for new home owners to hold house-warming parties. On these evenings, between dancing to the music of a concertina, each guest gave a solo performance of a favourite song or recital. Kerosene lamps and candles were not yet available, so lighting was provided by lamps containing muttonbird oil. Although they gave out sufficient light, they also produced a great deal of smoke. However, rather than break up a good party, the wicks were simply snuffed every hour or so until the smoke cleared and the festivities continued.

Dances were later held in the old schoolhouse after it was converted into a seed storage shed and were slightly more formal. The ladies, dressed in all their finery and wearing work shoes, slipped into their delicate dancing pumps upon arrival. When the dancing commenced the work shoes, stored on the overhead rafters, inevitably clobbered the merrymakers as they pounded the floor boards. After the Public Hall replaced the seed shed in 1936 it became the venue for dances, weddings, concerts and other community events. It also doubled as the local cinema, begun by Harry Woolnough and the Mitchell Film Committee in the late 1940s.

The concertinas, smoky oil lamps and seed shed have long gone, but the house-warming parties and sing-a-longs have not. Today, Islanders can be found pounding the floor boards at the Bowling Club dances and, on occasions, some merrymakers still get clobbered!

CRIMES AND MISDEMEANOURS

WILLIAM C. WHITING.

HUGH LANGWELL.

The first prison – after Captain Poole's oil barrel – was a ready made lock-up described as a large sentry box with a heavy bar and padlock. Despatched from Sydney in 1891 the Islanders refused to unload it and sent it back. However the authorities were not amused and had it returned, accompanied by several men to ensure its delivery. Erected in the eastern corner of Farnell Park it served as a storeroom for onions until residents were emphatically reminded of its true purpose, and ordered to remove their produce. It was then used for storage of farming equipment. The jail remained in situ until 1910, by which time the padlock had rusted and the key was long missing.

The next incarceration facility was established in 1985 when the presence of a resident law enforcer was finally considered necessary. The lock-up, contracted to a local builder, was to follow the construction of a police residence by Public Works Department builders. Upon completion of the house surplus building materials and equipment were sold off to a number of residents. However, the jail project was then delayed when it was discovered there was a serious lack of materials to build it with – the Islanders had unwittingly bought the cop shop! The 'stolen goods' were retrieved – except for the paint – which by then adorned the walls of several homes. The cell was finally built and immediately put to use to host poker evenings.

Nowadays in a world that seems to be riddled with crime, Lord Howe Island suffers its share. Court is occasionally convened at the Public Hall where visiting magistrates rule on offences that generally involve drink, drugs, clobberings (due to the former two) and traffic violations. However, felonies of an extreme nature are still few and far between. And Islanders still boast a time-honoured tradition of leaving keys in vehicles and their homes unlocked.

THE CROWN VS WILLIAM WHITING

The first Islander to appear in a Sydney court was William Whiting; charged with assault on Hugh Langwell – known to residents since he commissioned the 1911 Inquiry into the Kentia palm seed trade. The case was heard in the Central Police Court on 23 August 1916. According to Langwell's testimony, Whiting for no reason at all, jumped from his sled and struck him full force in the eye. As he lay on the ground quite dazed, his assailant proceeded to kick him repeatedly in the small of the back. It was then that Whiting challenged him to a punch-up. However, Langwell declined

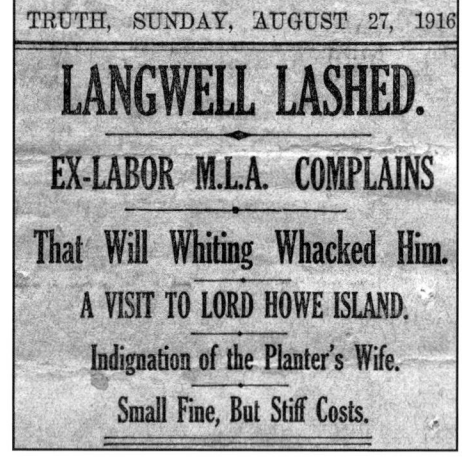

TRUTH, SUNDAY, AUGUST 27, 1916

LANGWELL LASHED.

EX-LABOR M.L.A. COMPLAINS

That Will Whiting Whacked Him.

A VISIT TO LORD HOWE ISLAND.

Indignation of the Planter's Wife.

Small Fine, But Stiff Costs.

due to the immediate state of his health! Whiting did not deny the charge and, in his testimony, said he was defending the honour of his wife, Susan, whom Langwell had constantly lusted after during her soirees and those hosted by her sisters.

Witnesses were called for both sides including Susan, who testified that Langwell had, indeed, told her he loved her and often made love to her with his eyes. Evidence of his infatuation with her was found in a book titled *Happy Hawkins*, in which Langwell had scribbled notes alluding to the seduction of Mrs Whiting. However, the evidence against Whiting proved too damning. With the Great War raging in Europe anti German sentiments were running high, and the kicking of a man when he was down was considered a *German trick*. William was callously likened by

Langwell to *an Englishman who would go to America, become naturalised, then go to war as a German and shoot his fellow man.*

William Whiting was found guilty and given 24 hours to pay the 1 shilling fine, £3.10s court cost and £17 damages to Hugh Langwell. Default meant three months imprisonment with hard labour. One of the most pertinent questions asked during cross-examination by Mr Windeyer, Counsel for the Plaintiff, was: -

Do they go joy-riding in sleds on Lord Howe?

A FOWL CASE

On a crisp autumn morning in May 1984, a big white rooster and a scrawny bantam sat side by side in separate cages at the Public Hall. Overhead, a large sign read 'NOT ME' with an arrow pointing to the larger bird. Next to it was written 'HIM' with an arrow indicating the bantam. And so the scene was set for an extraordinary court case.

The bantam was the cause of a noise pollution charge brought against Roseanne O'Brien (daughter of Norm and Daphne Simpson) by her neighbours, who owned a guest lodge. The rooster allegedly crowed at all hours of the night, making sleep difficult for the plaintiffs and their guests. Clarrie Briese, the presiding magistrate, and court officials were flown from Sydney for the three day case.

The bantam's 'trial' was played to a full house. The court was subjected to the plaintiffs' diary, detailing the minute-to-minute entries of when the cock crowed. Several 'expert' witnesses were called to testify in the bantam's defence, in which the life of a cock and other birds were intimately discussed. The outcome of the case was probably determined by the testimony of Gary Owens (married to Diane Wilson), the proprietor of another lodge. He informed the court that an elderly female guest upon hearing a rooster crow, wanted to know if it meant it was having sex! On adjourning the court on the second day, Magistrate Briese declared a 'hearing' of the bantam would be conducted at the scene of the crime early the following morning. He stressed that nobody but court officials be present.

Dawn came and with it many 'early risers' who learned just how many roosters there were on the Island! But, not a peep came from the bantam. As the tension rose, he was released into the henhouse where he silently mounted the nearest chook. This action prompted Magistrate Briese's audible comment – *well, that answers that lady's question.*

Back in court, there was jubilation when the bantam was found innocent, albeit at a cost of $25,000 to the Australian taxpayer. Undaunted by the court's decision, the plaintiffs vowed to have the rooster retried. However, before he could have his 'second day' in court the bantam was eaten by a dog.

TALES OF THE SEA

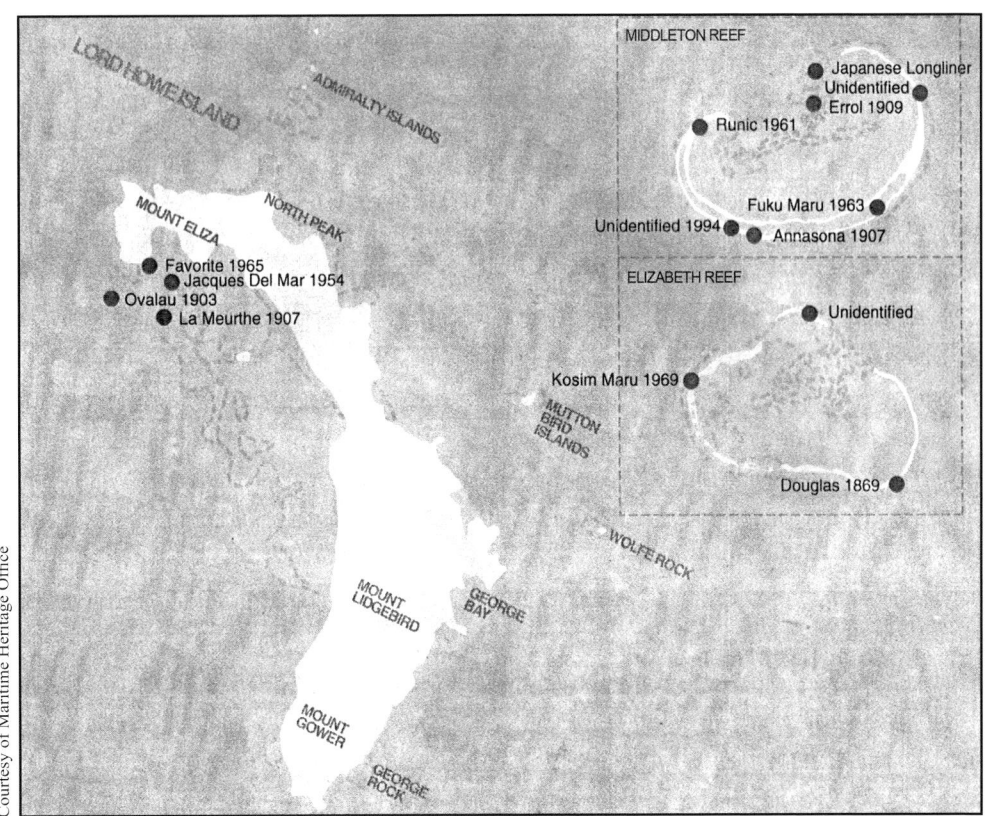

Shipwreck Sites

The first castaways on Lord Howe Island actually 'ran away' from the Tasmanian whaler *Runaway* in 1824. They were reported to have stayed for several months before being 'rescued' by a passing ship. The Island may have looked like paradise to the four deserters but without anyone else around – especially female company – they probably got on each other's nerves! From 1834 shipwrecked parties from as far away as Middleton Shoals were welcomed into the community. Hence, the testimonials hung by George Kirby on the schoolhouse walls during his time as teacher. Some shipwrecks have already been mentioned as being the source of new settlers.

A POT OF GOLD?

No history of an island can be complete without a legend of buried treasure, and the wreck of the whaler *George* gave Lord Howe its very own. What the treasure was and how the *George* acquired it has never been confirmed. The popular theory among whalers of the day was that it was payment received for double-cruising. It was believed the 185-ton Tasmanian ship took one or more loads of oil from the Middle Ground to Sydney, to sell to other vessels needing their quota before sailing home. A sum of £2500 was paid, most likely in gold or Spanish coin. While heading back to Hobart with a further cargo of oil, it was decided to refill the water casks at Lord Howe Island. As the *George* waited for the supplies to be brought on board, a heavy mist fell over the mountains and Captain Rattenbury mistook Mount Gower for Mount Lidgbird. The mistake resulted in the ship striking a rock. As she began to rapidly fill with water, the Captain and crew abandoned the vessel and rowed into a rocky inlet. In February 1831, after spending several weeks stranded in the bay, Rattenbury and four crewmen were rescued by the brig *Mary Elizabeth* when she called in for water. The remaining men were later picked up by the London whaler *Nelson.*

No mention of treasure was made in either ship's account of the rescue. However in December 1831, Captain Tregurtha of the barque *Caroline*, stated in his log: -

> Sailed from Hobart Town on a whaling voyage and shaped a course for Lord Howe's Island. My mate said he knew where the treasure was buried. On 15th December we sighted the Island and landed two quarter-boats. It took us seven hours to reach the shore, where we found a great number of bronzewing pigeons. We shot about seventy of them, but were unable to find the treasure, as the country seemed to have altered considerably, my mate said.

The rock the ship struck was given the name George Rock and the inlet was named Georges Bay. Over the decades, many conclusions have been drawn in respect of the 'treasure of Georges Bay'. They range from the highly sceptical – *it never existed*; the doubtful – *it will never be found*; to the Machiavellian – *the double-crossing swines who Rattenbury left behind shared the booty with the crew of the Nelson.* On the other hand, the observation by Tregurtha's mate that the *country seemed to have altered* suggests they may have been searching for it in the wrong bay. Perhaps the treasure still lies where it was buried – accruing interest while waiting to be found!

MUTINY

On 23 March 1842 the vessel *Water Witch* laid anchor at the Island. Chief Officer King was left in charge while Captain Christie, Surgeon Smith and a third mate went ashore to procure provisions. Twenty pigs and half a ton of potatoes, purchased from Captain Owen Poole, were sent off with Smith and the mate in two boats to the ship, with orders for King to keep the vessel near the Island during the night. Captain Christie stayed behind to pay for the merchandise. That was the last time *Water Witch* was seen for quite some time. Captain Christie remained on the Island until 13 May, when he and Captain Poole were advised to make a full report of the incident to the authorities in Sydney. *Water Witch* was then marked *a lawful prize for any British ship*. Suspicions were aroused in Newcastle on 6 June when a man calling himself 'Captain' King sought shipment to Sydney for a number of chests, and one Howe's Island pig. However, by the time the authorities arrived on the scene the ship was gone. She finally arrived back in Sydney of her own accord on 23 February 1843. In defence of his actions, Francis King claimed the crew forced him to take command of the ship. Although they were charged, *Water Witch* again disappeared and the case against the mutineers did not eventuate.

OTHER DISASTERS

The barque *Wolf*, carrying 1700 barrels of sperm oil (valued at £1600), was eighteen months out of Sydney when, on 8 August 1837, she anchored off Lord Howe to provision with that deadly necessity called water. At 1.00 pm she struck a rock, known now as Wolf Rock. The impact knocked her rudder off the stern post and carried away three pintles, allowing her to clear the rock. On sounding the pumps, Captain Evans found no water and assumed there was no damage to the bottom. He then gave orders to unship the rudder and set course for Sydney. However when the pumps were again sounded ten minutes later, there was four feet of water in the hold and rising. In desperation both pumps were immediately set to work but the damage was evident. Captain Evans then attempted to run her to Lord Howe, but at 4 pm he ordered the crew to abandon ship. Thirty minutes later *Wolf* capsized and sank ten miles from shore. On reaching the Island, Evans and his men waited four weeks before joining the whaler *Psyche*.

In his report of the incident, Evans wrote that they were treated with the greatest kindness by the few individuals on the Island who shared with them their garden produce and their last pound of flour.

In March 1849 the barque *Despatch*, bound from Sydney to London with a cargo of wool, caught fire 150 miles from the Island. It was soon out of control and the crew abandoned her. With twenty-one men in one boat and ten in another, they made a bid to reach Lord Howe. However, on the way the boats were separated. The crew of the smaller boat were picked up by the *Governor Burke* and taken to Sydney but there was no sign of the other. On 27 March *Rover's Bride* and *Prince George* were sent from

Jacques del Mar (1954)

Sydney in search of it. Upon reaching Lord Howe in severe weather conditions, it was learned that the men *had* reached the Island but, as food was scarce, they left just a few days before in an attempt to make it back to the Australian coast. Neither the boat nor its men were seen again.

On 8 May 1857 the whaler *Lady Blackwood*, six days out of Sydney, landed Captain Oliver and his family. Two days later, an upturned boat with several men clinging to it was sighted near North Reef. A search of the immediate area was hampered by heavy seas and strong winds. When conditions finally abated all that was found were two oars and a white flannel shirt. Fearing the worst, Captain Field accompanied Captain Oliver to the *Lady Blackwood* which they found abandoned and a lifeboat missing. It was assumed that as the weather deteriorated, *Lady Blackwood's* crew of six made a fatal decision to reach the safety of land. Their bodies were never recovered.

Bound for San Francisco with 1150 tons of coal, SM *Stetson* left Newcastle on 10 March 1877. Soon after, the vessel sprang a leak and although her pumps were going day and night she continued taking water. Finally the Captain decided to make the 300 mile run to Lord Howe and beach her. Three seamen, Alfred Brown, Charles Smith and Michael Fitzpatrick elected to take the ship's boat and try to reach Sydney. They made it in seven days. *Stetson* anchored off the Island on 24 March, but the following day an attempt to run her through the North Passage failed. She struck the reef and was holed. Captain Curtiss, his family and eleven crew were taken ashore. While waiting for a ship to take them back to Sydney, the Captain's young son, Evan, went missing. After several days he was found safe and well by 3 year-old Grace Nichols, in a dense palm forest where the Public Hall stands today.

The US Consul engaged Captain Amora to take the family and crew back to Sydney on the *Esperanza*. Amora later returned on the *Mary Peverley* to salvage as much of the *Stetson* as he could. However, he stayed so long that his men threatened mutiny. It was this incident that first brought Captain Armstrong to the Island.

When the trading steamer *Ovalau* anchored in the North Passage on 19 October 1903, a fire was reported in her cargo of copra. Unable to extinguish the flames, the crew quickly removed the passengers and closed the hatches. However as the last crewman escaped the ship, the forehead hatch blew out engulfing the ship in flames. A large quantity of pearl shell was reported to have been on board but, as the burned remains settled in a deep hole among the coral, it could not be recovered.

The *Maelgwyn* was 106 days out of Peru when, 600 miles east of Lord Howe, she was struck by a severe squall that carried away her masts and all but two of her boats. The storm shifted the ballast so that the ship rode on her side. With the keel visible to the crew, they continued riding in that position for three weeks before the Island was sighted on 27 January 1907. With sanctuary in reach, seven men manned the jollyboat and nineteen crammed into the lifeboat. The ship went down but not before the Captain salvaged the saloon's silver teapot, sugar basin and milk jug!

La Meurthe was an old French warship being towed from New Caledonia to Sydney. While sailing in a strong north-west wind near Lord Howe, she broke away from the vessel in charge. One man was killed when the cable snapped. A change of wind to the south-west then took her onto the Island's reef early in the evening of 9 October 1907. A three masted wooden vessel with auxiliary engine and copper fastened, *La Meurthe* was considered valuable to the Moreland Metal Company. The copper was said to have contained a small percentage of gold. With the assistance of Islanders, who received

£300 for their share of the salvage, she was stripped and the hull set on fire. Martha Nichols also acquired materials to build her new home, aptly named *La Meurthe* – and maybe she found her French lover in the process!

The *Whangaroa* was a schooner-rigged scow engaged in the New Zealand timber trade. On a trip to Sydney fully laden with a cargo of white pine, she sprang a leak early in the voyage. At first her pumps kept the water down, but after weathering a severe gale for several days she became water-logged. Although the pine cargo kept her afloat, the decks were awash and the crew were forced to live on a stage built on top of the deckhouse. The drinking water became unpalatable and the only food was rotting potatoes. Finally, on 23 June 1911 Lord Howe Island was sighted twenty-five miles away. A boat was launched from the stricken vessel and, after rowing all night, Captain Pearson and his crew reached land. They were met by James Tyrell and taken to the home of William Thompson where they remained for several weeks.

The force with which the *Makambo* struck a rock in 1918 caused its lights to go out, creating panic and confusion. As the crew tried to lower a lifeboat containing several passengers, the ropes jammed while it still hung in the davits. The ropes were cut and it dropped but luckily kept afloat. Unfortunately a woman was lost when she tried to jump into the boat, falling between it and the *Makambo*. Her body was not recovered.

Mystery Star was a 16 ft motor skiff used in a movie shot on Lord Howe called *Mystery Island*. Upon completion of the film two cast members, Brian Abbott and Lesley Hay Simpson, set out on the boat for Sydney on 6 October 1936. They carried 38 gallons of petrol and hoped to make the trip in eight days. When they failed to arrive, the destroyer *Waterhen,* two Seagull amphibian planes and a Gannet monoplane began an extensive ocean and coastal search, but they were not found.

Only a month later Gower Wilson, his son Jack, William Hamill and three others set out on their fatal voyage in Gower's newly built 32 ft launch *Viking*. Leaving Sydney on 1 November, the boat was reported to have passed South Head in a heavy sea at 5.15 pm. After ten days had elapsed and there was still no sign of the launch, HMAS *Vendetta* left Sydney to search for it. Norman Wallis followed in his yacht *Wanderer* and a number of trading vessels, including the *Morinda,* altered their course in order to pick up the supposed route of *Viking*. No trace was found. Fifteen years later at 1 am on 28 September 1951, *Viking* II passed South Head. Built to the same dimensions as *Viking,* she was owned by Gower's son Roy who, with a crew of three, reached Lord Howe Island on 3 October. According to Roy's wishes, upon his death in 1987 his body was laid to rest in the ocean that claimed his father and brother.

On 16 June 1951, Tom 'Count' Payten (son of Henry and Mabel) and Bryant 'Matches' Smythe (son of Harry and Elsie) risked adverse weather conditions to take a boat out fishing. They did not return. Despite an extensive search by other launches, and an RAAF Lincoln bomber, no trace of them was found. A month later, pieces of Tom's boat washed ashore on Little Island at the base of Mount Lidgbird.

Other vessels to come to grief at the Island were the American yacht *Bachelor's Bride* in September 1951, *Jacques-del-Mar* in 1954, *Reposado* in 1959, *Favourite* in 1965 and *Pacific Chieftain* in 1968.

BALLS PYRAMID

Marquis de Victor Henri Rochcfort was a French journalist and politician. In 1873 he was confined as a political prisoner to the penal colony in Noumea. In 1874 he and five other detainees, unhappy with the food, service, comfort and lack of consideration shown by their landlord, developed a firm resolve to escape their lodgings! This was achieved with the assistance of an enterprising Australian sea captain – to whom they promised a substantial cash reward. The voyage to Newcastle with Captain Law on the *Peace Comfort and Ease,* took the escapees past Lord Howe Island and Balls Pyramid, of which Rochefort wrote: -

> In the course of the four hundred league journey from Noumea, the only distraction from the monotonous rhythm of the 'symphony in blue major' known as the Pacific Ocean had been our passing by Lord Howe Island, which is overlooked from a height of five hundred metres by the dark shelf known as Ball's Pyramid, which seems to threaten nearby ships but in fact warns them, thus combining the useful and the disagreeable.
>
> As we passed this monument, erected (as a Freemason would say) by the Great Architect of the Universe, and which is reminiscent of an enormous feudal castle once occupied by some sea-monster – perhaps Adamastor whose place of residence Camöens has not revealed to us – the captain of the P.C.E. told us that in 1853 four men who were shipwrecked when their boat broke up on the coral surrounding Lord Howe Island had lived for two months on this block of granite. Their only food had been the eggs of seagulls, speckled kestrels and mallemucks which they would pluck from the

Pyramid (drawing by Henri Rochefort)

crevices of the pyramid where these hardy birds had nested.

We saw what looked to be not so much a cloud as a winged waterspout whirling above this Tower of Doom. By the look of things, however, the four above-mentioned travellers had not eaten all the eggs in the henhouse.

Perhaps the good Captain Law was just adding a little 'oomph' to the rhythm of that symphony in blue major. However, while no records could be found of anyone ever being stranded on the Pyramid, there is no evidence to the contrary. Although not shipwrecked, several people have since landed on and climbed the Pyramid – including that intrepid adventurer, Dick Smith.

A GRAVEYARD OF SHIPS

Middleton Reef, 192 kms north of Lord Howe, was discovered by Lieutenant John Shortland on the *Alexander* in 1788. He named it after Admiral Charles Middleton. Forty-eight kms to its south lies Elizabeth Reef. At times known as Seringapstam, Clark or Eliza Reef, its existence was first recorded in 1820, but it was not officially named until 1831 after it claimed the brig *Elizabeth*. It is believed that as many as ninety ships may have met their doom on these treacherous shoals that form part of the Lord Howe Rise. Of the thirty-eight known wrecks, twenty-six ships have been identified. Despite a recorded loss of more than fifty lives, most shipwrecked crews survived.

The brig *Naiad* was wrecked on Elizabeth Reef on 9 July 1885. Some of the crew abandoned the ship and set a course for Sydney. Over two weeks later they saw Lord Howe but at first made no attempt to reach it. Luckily for the crew, Islanders spotted them, sent a boat out and persuaded them to come ashore. The *Naiad's* boat was heavily laden and would not have survived the strong south-west wind that sprang up that same night. The remaining crew of the *Naiad* was rescued by the *Mary Ogilvie*.

The barque *Annasona*, bound for Australia from Peru, struck Middleton Reef on the evening of 18 January 1907. Captain Blackstock threatened to shoot any of his crew who attempted to lower the boats before daylight. They took heed – and all thirty men reached the safety of Lord Howe where they joined twenty-six castaways from the *Maelgwyn*. Norman Wallis, known to many Islanders, bought the wreck of the *Annasona* for 5 shillings in 1936.

THE BRITISH NAVY RETURNS!

HMS *Supply* accidentally found the Island on 17 (or 18!) February 1788. A 170-

ton warship that carried 8 guns and a crew of 50, she was the armed tender for the flagship of the First Fleet.

HMS *Nottingham*, accidentally *found* Lord Howe Island on 7 July 2002. A Type 42 destroyer with a complement of 253 – a 50 metre gash was torn in her hull when she struck Wolf Rock while manoeuvring to allow a helicopter to land on the deck. With five compartments flooded, the 3500 tonne ship lay at anchor at the Island for several weeks until completely pumped out. Most of her personnel were transported by RAAF Hercules to Richmond air base. However, those who stayed behind were afforded the same hospitality as the castaways of a by-gone era. The *Nottingham* was towed to Newcastle and later transported to England on the Dutch heavy lifting ship *Swan.* She returned to sea after extensive repairs to her hull and electrical system were carried out at a cost of $A102 m.

Following a naval enquiry in which Commander Farrington was sentenced to a court martial reprimand, he said: -

> This incident reminds us all that the sea is an unforgiving master and all those who follow this rewarding profession must treat it with respect, regardless of the technology that might be available.

HMS Nottingham at Lord Howe Island

THE LAST WORD

Sunday School Scripture lessons taught Garth, 'Widge' Fenton and me that Jesus Christ was crucified on a faraway hill called Calvary. Nonsense! Everyone knew that He lived on Lord Howe Island and, as a very large man, was nailed to the cross carved by His very large dad on the rock-face of Mount Lidgbird. He then ascended into Heaven, which was a big place at the top of the mountains. Just who killed Him, we were not quite sure, but suspicious glances were cast upon anyone who looked about 2000 years old. In our innocence, Lord Howe Island encompassed the universe – there was simply no other place. Of course, we have since been enlightened, but it is still hard to believe that Heaven exists anywhere but at the top of those silent sentinels.

Our childhood – in a time betwixt the old and the new – was uncomplicated. Milking cows, feeding chooks, fattening pigs for Christmas, gathering kindling for chip heaters, chopping wood for fuel stoves and cutting newspaper squares for dunny paper were still part of Island life. We rode to school on push-bikes in all kinds of weather. (There were no cars to drive us). Besides the chores, there was the excitement of watching the flying boats, the scramble for newspapers dropped from Neptune Bombers (consigned to the dunny once read), launch trips on ship days and Sunday picnics with our mates, when the treasured moments of youth were captured on the old Box Brownie.

As a fifth generation Islander from the Andrews line, I was fascinated by the stories and anecdotes related by past generations. The tales they told inspired my passion to write a history on the people of Lord Howe. The task was supported by my family and peers, who hold with me the same pride in our heritage, instilled in us by our forebears. I also had the support of friends who have 'done their time in purgatory' to acquire Islander status; and share our interest in the Island's past – as well as its uncertain future.

The journey into the 20th century was, indeed, wild and bumpy – but the hopes and dreams of the first settlers, and the love of their Island home, was the seatbelt that secured them on their ride. Their story can be summed up by the following quote from Canadian poet, George Woodstock: -

Pioneers did not produce original works of art, because they were creating human environments; they did not imagine utopias, because they were shaping them.

REFERENCES

America Activities in the Central Pacific, 1790-1870, Vol. 4, a history, geography and ethnography pertaining to American involvement and Americans in the Pacific taken from contemporary newspapers etc. edited by Gerard Ward. Courtesy Michael Dyer, New Bedford Whaling Museum

American Whalers and Traders in the Pacific: a guide to records on microfilm, Part 111, an Index to places visited, edited by Robert Langdon. Australian National Maritime Museum

An Historical Journal of Events at Sydney and at Sea, 1787-1792, Captain John Hunter, Mitchell Library

Archeology of Whaling in Southern Australia and New Zealand, edited by Susan Lawrence and Mark Stanforth/Australasian Society for Historical Archaeology and Australian Institute for Maritime Archaeology pp 87-92 – Special Publication No. 10 Bolga Press

Australian Geographic Book of Lord Howe Island, Ian Hutton

Barney Genealogical Record of Chase Family, Nantucket History Association

Birds of Lord Howe Island, Ian Hutton

Captain Armstrong Re Lord Howe Island, Mitchell Library

Earl Howe: Smith Elder & Co's Dictionary of National Biography, Mitchell Library

Federation on Meteorology: Trevor Donald tells it all: Life in the Bureau from to 1947 to 1989

Fitzgerald, R D., letters to Sydney Morning Herald, 6 January 1877, 12 January 1877 and Sydney Mail, 13 February 1877, courtesy Les King

Henri Rochefort: Noumea to Newcastle, Story of an Escape

Henry Lidgbird Ball, Bodwick transcripts, vol 1, Mitchell Library

Historical Whaling Records from the West Indian Ocean, Phoebe Wray & Kenneth R Martin, Australian National Maritime Museum

Historic Nantucket, courtesy Elizabeth Oldham, Nantucket Historical Association

History of Lord Howe Island, A; Max Nicholls

In the Heart of the Sea, story of the Essex, Nathanial Philbrick

Journal of James Scott, Sergeant of Marines, Mitchell Library

Journal of Philip Gidley King, Lieutenant R N, 1787-1790, Mitchell Library

Journals of Captain James Cook on his voyages of discovery: voyage of the Endeavour 1768-1771, Australian Maritime Museum

John Bowie Wilson, Thomas Richards Govt. printer 1885, Mitchell Library

Lord Howe Island 1788-1988, bicentennial publication

Lord Howe Island 1882, John Bowie Wilson

Lord Howe Island, Harold Rabone

Lord Howe Island REP – Heritage Study, Final report to the LHI Board, Birmingham, J., Kelly, M., Tanner, H., 1984

Lord Howe Island School Magazine 1968

On the Rim of a Volcano, Early Adventism on Lord Howe Island, Milton Hook Pinetrees, Lord Howe Island 1842-1992 – a brief history of the Andrews-Nichols-Kirby families, Kerry McFadyen

Plants, Seeds and Specimens Received at Government Botanic Garden February 1880 to December 1898, Les King

Report of the Royal Commission of Inquiry into the Condition and Welfare of the Residents of Lord Howe Island, 1912, family documents

School Centenary, Lord Howe Island, 1879-1979

Scurvy: How a Surgeon, a Mariner and a Gentleman Solved the Greatest Medical Mystery of the Age, Stephen R Brown

South Sea Whaler, the - an annotated bibliography and published historical literary and art material relating to whaling in the Pacific Ocean in the nineteenth Century, Appendix 2 – the major whaling grounds of the Pacific Ocean, compiled by Honore Forster, Kendall Whaling Museum, Mass.

Whaling Logbooks & Journals 1613-1927, an inventory of manuscript records in public collections, compiled by Stuart C. Sherman, prepared by A. Howard Clark in 1887, Australian National Maritime Museum

ACKNOWLEDGMENTS

A very special thanks must go to the following: -

For their support in more ways than one – Joy Davies, Bill Shead, Marion Steiner, Angus Watt and Peter Heck.

For editorial assistance – my sister-in-law Sue, my wonderful sons Brett and Mark, Sandy Corcoran and Sarah Baker.

For computer assistance, a device I still cannot master – Kate Tait, Jo Trentini and Jackie Watt, who defeated the 'red man'.

Graphic Designer, typist and now a Lord Howe Island fan – a very patient Alan Knott.

For photographs and scanning – Bond Imaging, Joern Harris (the seventh generation children), Ian Hutton, Hazel Payten, Pinetrees and the LHI Historical Society and for his cartoons – Mark Rowley.

For family and other information – Thelma Wilson, Gai Wilson, Darcel Nobbs, Ray Shick, Les and Dulcie King, Ginny and Bill Retmock, Linda Retmock, Betty Elliott, Lorraine de Russet, Deanna Harvey, Larry Wilson, Barney and Garth Nichols, Tas Douglass, Esven Fenton, Kerry and Kate McFadyen, Don and Una Payten, Ysobel Heffernan, Hazel and Vicki Payten, Lance Wilson, Clive Wilson, Mavis Fitzgerald, Patty Dignam, Sandra Beaumont, Stan Nichols, Robyn Allen.

To all at 'The Summit' – Lyn and John Davis and Gina Fay for letting me trash their computer, and Jess and Sam for their canine company.

The Lagoon, Mount Lidgbird and Mount Gower